BEFORE THE STORM
TAKES IT AWAY

Also by Gaylord Brewer

POETRY

Worship the Pig (2020)
The Feral Condition (2018)
Country of Ghost (2015)
Give Over, Graymalkin (2011)
The Martini Diet (2008)
Let Me Explain (2006)
Exit Pursued by a Bear (2004)
Barbaric Mercies (2003)
Four Nails (2001)
Devilfish (1999)
Presently a Beast (1996)

FICTION

Octavius the 1st (2008)

CREATIVE NONFICTION

The Poet's Guide to Food, Drink, & Desire (2015)

LITERARY CRITICISM

Charles Bukowski (1997)
*Laughing like Hell: The Harrowing Satires
    of Jim Thompson* (monograph, 1996)
David Mamet and Film (1993)
*A Detective in Distress: Philip Marlowe's
    Domestic Dream* (monograph, 1989)

BEFORE THE STORM TAKES IT AWAY

brief nonfiction

ॐ

*hymns to morning & night, tempest & augury,
travel, scandal, silence, bucolic & domestic bliss,
sheltering in place, name-dropping the dead,
bird geeking, libations & cookery, immovable
feasts, the poetry biz, a world pandemic, selling
the year for a song, & two damn good dogs*

GAYLORD BREWER

 Red Hen Press | *Pasadena, CA*

Book design by Mark E. Cull

Library of Congress Cataloging-in-Publication Data
Names: Brewer, Gaylord, 1965– author.
Title: Before the storm takes it away: brief nonfiction / Gaylord Brewer.
Description: First edition. | Pasadena, CA: Red Hen Press, 2024. | "hymns to morning & night, tempest & augury, travel, scandal, silence, bucolic & domestic bliss, sheltering in place, name-dropping the dead, bird geeking, libations & cookery, immovable feasts, the poetry biz, a world pandemic, selling the year for a song, & two damn good dogs"
Identifiers: LCCN 2023040163 (print) | LCCN 2023040164 (ebook) | ISBN 9781636281360 (paperback) | ISBN 9781636281377 (e-book)
Subjects: LCGFT: Literature.
Classification: LCC PS3552.R4174 B44 2024 (print) | LCC PS3552.R4174 (ebook) | DDC 814/.6—dc23/eng/20231206
LC record available at https://lccn.loc.gov/2023040163
LC ebook record available at https://lccn.loc.gov/2023040164

The National Endowment for the Arts, the Los Angeles County Arts Commission, the Ahmanson Foundation, the Dwight Stuart Youth Fund, the Max Factor Family Foundation, the Pasadena Tournament of Roses Foundation, the Pasadena Arts & Culture Commission and the City of Pasadena Cultural Affairs Division, the City of Los Angeles Department of Cultural Affairs, the Audrey & Sydney Irmas Charitable Foundation, the Meta & George Rosenberg Foundation, the Albert and Elaine Borchard Foundation, the Adams Family Foundation, Amazon Literary Partnership, the Sam Francis Foundation, and the Mara W. Breech Foundation partially support Red Hen Press.

First Edition
Published by Red Hen Press
www.redhen.org

Acknowledgments

Grateful acknowledgment is made to the editors of the following publications, where many of these pieces initially appeared, often in slightly different forms.

Aji Magazine: "Dyea, Alaska, Doesn't Even Exist"; *Another Chicago Magazine* ("Dispatch from a Pandemic"): "Advice on Weeding in Face of a Virus Pandemic and Plummeting World Markets," "Panic Baking at the End of the World: Upside-Down Cake with Rum and Fresh Pineapple"; *Broad River Review*: "Suicide"; *Caesura*: "Aubade with Wildlife and a Promise of Autumn," "Mask"; *Chautauqua*: "Montmartre, 1986"; *Clarestory*: "Coming Home from the Georgia Coast, Late Summer," "End of Days," "The Marshall House"; *El Portal*: "Notes on the Closing Year"; *Emrys Journal*: "Boudin of Longing, Kielbasa of Despair"; *Freshwater*: "The Beemer and the Doe," "Home Birding," "Nocturne"; *Front Range Review*: "Call of the White One," "Kingsley Amis and the Fanboy," "Origin Story, Jasper," "Shame"; *GreenPrints*: "Advice on Weeding in Face of a Virus Pandemic and Plummeting World Markets," "Bounty," "Last Blooms"; *The Iconoclast*: "Gloriously Alone"; *Kestrel*: "Fawn," "In All of Human History," "Talking to My Father"; *Metonym Journal*: "The Poets' Global Advocacy Group against Noise and Light Pollution"; *Negative Capability*: "Blood Loaf: Ghoulish Limit of Culinary Taste? Hell No!"; *Number One*: "Arthur Smith's Audience of One," "Famous Poet of the Midnight Sun," "First Day of School, 1971," "'Something there is that doesn't love a wall,'" "Still Not Illegal, Not Yet a Sin"; *Poetry East*: "Actual Winter Morning"; *Shift: A Journal of Literary Oddities*: "Reindeer Games"; *Shift* (MTSU Write): "The Solace of the Future"; *Skylight 47* (Ireland): "Last Words for Now," "Note to Samuel Pepys"; *Sugar House Review*: "Advice on Burning Manuscripts"; *Thin Air*: "Blackberries"; *Tojo Journal*: "Friday the 13th, Harvest Moon," "Sept. 1st, Sunday, 12:18 p.m.," "Shelter from the Storm," "Yellow Sky."

"Darkness," "In Time of Crisis and Quarantine, the Insistence of Small Things," "*Manoir Sur-le-Cap*," and "Tomorrow Would Be a Long Day" appeared in the anthology *The Power of the Pause: The Wonder of Our Here & Now* (Decatur, GA: Wising Up Press, 2022).

Thanks to Ron McFarland for introducing me to Gary Soto's *What Poets Are Like*, one of several coincidences that stirred the possible stew of this book. Thanks also to John Dufresne. I wrote "Dyea, Alaska, Doesn't Even Exist" at his request for a proposed collection of essays on, as I recall, places writers had fallen in love with at first sight. I'm fickle as far as that subject goes, but I enjoyed writing the Alaska piece, which was finished long before I envisioned this book. It, too, got me thinking. The essay may seem like an outlier here, but may I suggest that, rather, it's the linchpin, the fulcrum for the whole.

Last note: It's also coincidence that *Before the Storm Takes It Away* became my "COVID-19 book." In the summer of 2019, I was taking a breather from writing poetry and decided as an experiment to write ten short essays each month for a year. Then March 2020 arrived, bringing our altered world with it. (I still wonder at the odd feeling of trepidation and displacement throughout the preceding winter that I couldn't fully explain or define. *Viz.*, what follows.) Corollary to subsequent events is that this book is a bit of an anomaly, written in its entirety at the house in Tennessee. We're still not going out much.

Harvey Brewer—
1932–2021

Contents

I: Summer

II: *Autumn*

III: Winter

IV: Spring

Coda

BEFORE THE STORM
TAKES IT AWAY

I: SUMMER

Piemonte; world on fire; deadheading; dog origin stories; advice on burning manuscripts; sex with a horse; Finland; blood loaf; first day of school; hoorah for Hollywood

End of Days

What a dinner Monica has prepared for us. First, she and Allesandro and the younger couple with the baby girl, bowls of snacks and a glass of local red wine in the shade of the towering fig tree. When the family leaves for its dinner reservation—silly youth—we are escorted to our single candlelit table for two on the terrace. Allesandro uncorks a bottle of special barbera, only ten bottles remaining in his cellar. Then we begin: veal meatballs in zucchini cream; homemade agnolotti in a delightful plate with fifteen indentations—three small pastas in each space, rotating five different preparations/sauces so we may "try them all"; mustard-encrusted medallions of pork, pink and tender, alongside a thick slice of crispy pear; layered meringues dotted with fresh raspberries. As we finish dessert, Allesandro returns with two flutes, a complementary bottle of sparkling moscato. We toast our absurd fortune and safe return, drink one glass, then I enter the house, the kitchen, to see if our new friends would like to join us. They would. An hour of genial and bubbly conversation. They apologize repeatedly for their perfectly passable English, praise Claudia's "authentic" Italian accent, and invite us to join them in Thailand in January for yoga and a very different lifestyle. Brilliant. Absolutely. Why in the world not?

Our last night in the Piemonte—a fact I may have casually mentioned to them earlier—following a lazy day of just the two of us. No driving today, *grazie*. A late breakfast of jams and toast and cheese and coffee, then a walk up to the village, randomly in time for a noon procession of priest and congregation around the square: incantation of verse and song, the boy's gently swinging censer, the girl in white's trail of rose petals. Then afternoon by the long, narrow pool built for a committed swimmer—Monica, I suspect—a lovely, inviting pool approached through a canopy of wisteria, bordered by warm brick, surrounded by grass, overlooking a valley of vines and hazelnut trees. Above us the languid, buttery, ferocious sun. Tomorrow would be a day of calculated minutes, inevitable small errors, situations beyond our control, and already I feel the stress arriving in my fingertips and shoulders and breath. But hold it off; hold it off. Hold it off for the cool shadows of the room, a nap on the exquisite hand-carved bed while Claudia finishes her novel on the balcony. Hold it off when I join her to finish my own, so to pack the story away. I am caught off guard by the emotion the last pages bring. Somehow, the surprise tears feel right, joyful, a bit silly. But now it's time to shower, put on that last clean shirt, saved just in case, and join everyone at the table beneath the fig, evening just begun.

Fête de l'Indépendence

A dozen years past already. I'd been writing poems at a retreat in the Languedoc and then traveled north to meet a group of exchange students arriving for a month in Cherbourg. Most of them had never been out of the US before, a few never out of Tennessee. I wasn't officially in the fledgling program, was just a spouse hanger-on and general rah-rah supporter, and spent my days adding bits of comfort to our spartan apartment and cleaning grime from its floor-to-ceiling windows that became my curse. I would take a bus to the pier and wander the streets. Cherbourg's charms were, let us say, elusive. They had to be sought out. In the evenings, the only time my wife and I theoretically had alone, I'd often cook, and, nearly as often, a particular faculty member, uninvited, would knock on the door at dinnertime and settle in for a long and loud visit. Solitary time to think and write was rare, an unpleasant shock from my leisurely, productive weeks in the mountains.

I did quite a few favors for both students and staff and felt increasingly peevish, unthanked, and underappreciated. So I skipped the Fourth of July farewell party—the gray burgers, sweaty beer, paper flags, provisional tattoos of liberty. I was leaving alone the next morning on an early train to Paris to fly home. My rations were one fat rabbit liver sautéed in olive oil and butter made from the cream of Normandy cows, the remains of the morning's baguette, and a last half bottle of red wine from the stash I'd brought with me from the South. I had the cavernous room all to myself, for the moment, and blowing something up sounded utterly enchanting.

Climate

Every midsummer morning, old man shuffling in his garden, I deadhead the mush of the previous day's lilies and toss the handfuls of goo into a plastic bin. Lately, the heat is a physical assault when one steps through the front door. Before the five-minute chore is complete, my T-shirt is dark against my chest, my feet slippery inside my clownish slippers. I blink up into the blinding, bullying sky, dazed and surrendered. It is 8:30 a.m.; the mercury in the old thermometer (in the shade) reads 81°F and rising, too hot already to walk Lucy to the creek. Four days ago, the town of Carpentras in southeastern France, a town I know, reached 44°C (112°F). The photos looked bleached out, overexposed, something from a story of apocalypse.

Our Virginia Peck daylily bed is our pride, our history, and our burden. Most of the flowers have been gifts over the past two decades, an accrued legacy. Traditionally, the explosion of blooms is the last week of June and the first of July, weeks I've planned many holidays around. As I mistakenly did this year, to return on June 24 to a bed already peaked. In the last half dozen years, the season has shifted, I'd estimate, at least ten days earlier into the calendar, maybe two weeks. We had a Scarlock lily on May 31, for god's sake. Unprecedented. Canary in the coal mine.

July 2. I stand sticky with sweat tallying a total of eighty-nine, this number inflated by the stalwart late producers Cherry Cheeks and Bengaleer. Back in the day—again, the fairly recent day—today could have peaked at 150 flowers or more. A profusion of color, height, variation of petal, pistil, and stamen. Instead: Jesse James bloomed out yesterday; today the end for Scottsboro; Red Tart finished tomorrow. The bed's still gorgeous, a joy, and sexy as hell, although all those bare, browning scapes won't be ignored. Perhaps you think I'm overreacting, that this alteration of dates is no seismic shift and requires merely an adjustment in habit and thought? I am here to tell you otherwise. What remains: two Fran Dean, six Cordelia, seven Gay Cravat, two Added Dimensions, four Cranberry Rose, three Pearl Lewis, two Queen of Roses, four White Tie Affair, three Warner House, twelve Cherry Cheeks, five Light Loisteen, three Heady Wine, three Golden Prize, six Jog On, twelve Bengaleer, one Scottsboro, six Smokehouse Gold, eight Hudson Valley.

And fewer tomorrow. The day after that, with a projected temperature of 96°F, our national celebration of the sky on fire.

Origin Story, Jasper

In graduate school, I lived in a suburb of Columbus several miles north of Ohio State's sprawling campus and what we lovingly referred to as its "student ghetto." My preferred drive to school took me past an otherwise unremarkable pet food and supply store in a forgettable strip mall. The problem was the shop owners had concocted a deal with the Humane Society: the former's back room would house all the local puppies up for adoption, boxes full of fuzzy, bewildered siblings or individual strays with elliptical but heartbreaking narratives of separation or abandonment.

A wiser young man would have sought an alternate route to work or moved closer to town. Stopping by the store once or twice each week to tussle with the new arrivals was a dangerous game to play. I hadn't had a dog since I was a kid—i.e., since when my mother did the clean-up—and wasn't particularly in the market for one, especially a puppy, with the patience and training (and dribbling mayhem) involved.

One morning, in transit to a busy day in Denney Hall of teaching—or what passed for same—composition, followed by office hours and an afternoon seminar in Restoration Comedy, I was kneeled down in the damned puppy room, having a romp with a frisky Chow. I had also petted and introduced myself to a pretty American Eskimo—thin and alert and glowing white. (The short fur would later fill out to a majestic fluff.) The latter's handwritten sign: "Age: six months. Reason for adoption: owner can no longer take care of him." A skimpy narrative that spoke of a whole lost world.

I remember lifting the Chow back into its pen, naïvely about to stand and be on my way to the rigors of pedagogy and cultural theory, when the Eskimo, somehow having freed itself from the kennel—this is how I remember it—walked calmly and directly over. He stopped right in front of me, smiling, those beautiful ears pointed upward, and I never had a chance. As we both waited there, suspended between our lives before and after that moment, he gave a sly sideways look, very clearly as if to say:

What's the problem, dude? Let's get out of here! We only have fourteen years!

Kingsley Amis and the Fanboy

I'd been a huge admirer since I was an undergraduate. *Lucky Jim*, of course, but *Take a Girl Like You, Jake's Thing, That Uncertain Feeling, One Fat Englishman, Stanley and the Women*—I'd read and loved them all. That brittle English skewering of academic and bourgeois vanities, of our sexual mores adaptable to opportunity. Always, ultimately, a moralist's price to pay for faithlessness. And funny as all hell.

My first chapbook of poems, *Zócalo*, was coming out from a micropress, immortality chugging into the station at last. The short collection consisted of terse, imagistic pieces, guarded and moody, thematically centered around the town square of Cuernavaca, Mexico. Something like that. There wasn't much to it, and what was there wasn't much good. In other words, ideal material to send uninvited, with request for a supporting blurb, to the great British humorist. Where I'd acquired the poor man's address, I have no idea.

Amis was nearing seventy. He'd won the Booker a year or two earlier for *The Old Devils*, swan song in a career winding down. His health, I learned later, was by then in decline. I imagine him opening the afternoon mail, a second or third Bloody Mary—with lemon and an alchemical dash of ketchup, as he preferred—in one hand, while blinking at the curious artifact of my letter and manuscript in the other, the presumptuousness of my having sent the package exceeded, perhaps, only by the absolute inappropriateness of the solicitation. Amis had decades before written several volumes of metered verse, yes. He was a friend of Larkin, yes. But these little free-verse doodles oddly spaced across the pages would have been in no language he recognized or cared to.

And yet: Sir Kingsley wrote me back. What a small, lovely courtesy! The ordeal of typing out the note, signing his name in a contained hand, sealing and posting it. The half sheet of stationery—long since lost, unfortunately—printed simply "c/o 22 Prince Albert Road" across the top. The tenor of the short reply was obvious enough, but the wording kind. He thanked me for my thoughtfulness in writing him but admonished himself that he understood "nothing of contemporary poetry and must decline. With best wishes, yours sincerely."

Boudin of Longing, Kielbasa of Despair

That summer corn I just double-cut for the freezer. The rough husks, resistant silks, ethereal white kernels and sweet "milk" of the blade caressed along the cob. My hands a dripping mess. It's an easy poem. For the "turning," I might introduce my stocked freezer as a whimsical symbol of privilege, or maybe invoke the winter one must always prepare for, possibly an image of Grandma Brewer deaf and half blind over her stove. God forbid, stir in some polemic on industrial agriculture, local farmers. Maybe just a skillet, butter, and salt, keep it sensual and tasty.

Or forget the corn, already stacked in the cold atop last week's fava beans. (Favas, with their elaborate double-shelling, lend well to the poem of lonely ritual, of patience in appetite.) How about some verses concerning my slippers damp from the morning dew? Or speaking long distance to my mother last night about the brief, teasing storms that interrupt their months of drought and sadness? Or the disgruntled angle of my new reading glasses upside down on the end table? A single dark feather on the gravel drive. A spill of something unknown on the counter brought to the lips on a fingertip. A cross drawn on the dusty mirror. An empty bottle of wine. Wherever you look, really.

I've not written verse in more than a year. The sun rises and sets. The moon waxes and wanes. The dog still loves me if my pocket is full of biscuits. I've noted no change in my radiant disposition. I'm sure I'll come around, the old circus of womb-to-grave compelling another shot at the balloons, a rigged chance for the big prize! Only my wife has noticed or seems in the least concerned. I suspect she believes that the ritual is regenerative for me, that writing poems makes me a healthier and happier man, closer to self-fulfillment—*viz.*, easier to live with—one stanza at a time. Perhaps she's right. Pick your coarse or smooth grind, decide your level of heat and spice, opt for a natural or synthetic casing, then crank the handle. How the sausage is made. Life's mostly metaphor, anyway.

Advice on Burning Manuscripts

A simple charcoal grill for a simple task works best, rickety and self-assembled. Bear in mind a manuscript of even moderate ambition makes a dense sheaf, so an igniting fluid will be necessary. Set beloved pages gently onto the grate, douse liberally, and touch each corner with a struck match. Take your time. No urgency is required, no violence beyond the awaking flame itself. A ritual of release, not revenge. The intimate, irremediable act. Sip your beverage of choice and squint through coruscating fumes as the autumn night descends. (It is, of course, October, month of regret, reflection, and sorcery.)

As top pages, transmogrified, curl into the twilight like black moths, and a simmering, steady heat caresses the body of work, cover with the lid. Your part is done. Trust fire now to bring the words to their inarguable conclusion.

In my twenties, I burned a novel and witnessed its conflagration. *The Death of Auguste Rodin.* Indeed. Days later, I followed with my entire folder of short stories. Fourteen. No carbons, no files, no discs, no jump drives. Students tend to stare incredulously when I sometimes conjure those sweet moments. No exhilaration, no fervor, certainly no regret. Just a settling calm, the confidence of a right thing, as ragged tissues of ghosts silently rose in the chill of evening. Embers, aglow on their grave, sputtering a few last, spent words.

SeaWorld Armistice

James Doyle told me a story of once spotting Bukowski at Sea-World in San Diego. To make matters worse, the Dirty Old Man himself was carrying a large stuffed animal, perhaps an orca. The nearest racetrack a world away, any rescuing dive bar even farther. One recalls the poem in *War All the Time* when the mail carrier catches the poet watering the lawn and the two share a laugh: "Yeah, Harry, I know: / just an old man with a hose . . ."

Conjuring the scene pleases me immensely. There, amidst the Dolphins Encounter and Sea Lions Live, the Shipwreck Rapids and Tidal Twister, the Penguin House, corn dogs, and fruit smoothies, the two men sharing a look. Doyle said Bukowski gave a little grin, pointed a thumb and forefinger gun at him and dropped the trigger. *Got me. Busted.*

I don't believe Buk ever wrote of this oblique encounter, but Jim later did. He composed a delightful poem and, for some reason, dedicated it to me.

Montmartre, 1986

The rendering itself, competent in charcoal pencil, long since yellowed in a tube in a dusty attic corner, is likely lost for good. But the photo remains, and it turns out the photo is the fun part. Who snapped this image of young Brewer and his sketch artist, I've no idea, but the narrative's in the layers. Of what significance the actual drawing? The act of the commission, the dead-seriousness of the sit—that's our story.

The entire perimeter of the photo, however, pulls the curtain back even farther on the wizard's artifice: two other tourists also being sketched, an assembly line of posterity hinted just out of the frame. One girl looks amused, far from our man's somber intensity, and for whom this is no game. With the occasional serendipity of the cheap camera, the photo focuses sharply only on its background minutiae, while both the artist and our subject appear hazy, suggestively indistinct, as if fading already to their respective fates.

Blow the photo up, and the effect's even better. The others disappear. It is just Brewer staring his destiny down hard. The shadowed eyes, pursed lips, clench of jaw. The silhouette of black beret—oh yes!—and upturned collar of denim. Portrait of the Artist as a Young Man. He's only sixty years too late, after all. What the hell. An intense, handsome fellow. In fact, does he not resemble more than a little, even uncannily, Papa's famous passport photo of 1923? There's plenty of time still to beat on, a boat against the current. And if not, well . . . he looks damn good.

As you can tell, the photo doesn't elicit from me the cringing you would correctly assume it once did. Too much time in that foundering boat? I can't imagine what's on this guy's mind as he's happily borne back into the past, et cetera. But it's summer, it's Paris, and it seems churlish not to like the kid. In our close-up, of the sketch artist we see only the slender and spectral hands, one clutching his pad firm to the easel, the other, having roughed in the contour of the boy's head, now executing the remarkable details. Doing his job.

Bounty

A hot wet spring yielded small strawberries, intensely sweet. We ate gallons of them—in homemade ice cream or over fresh warm shortcake, sure, but mostly right out of the bowl, each glowing berry raised by its stem and devoured—every day in May we could get them. Bought either just-picked at Pearcy's Mercantile, when the sign was out, or two miles down the road directly in their field, chosen from among the three or four buckets the grandfather gave his back to that morning.

Now, in mid-July, strawberries are a sigh of memory, fava beans are finished, the asparagus in the garden has gone to seed. Our subject, our timely obsession, is peaches. This week I ate the last Red Haven, ate it in the proper manner, over the sink, the golden flesh dripping from chin and hand. After two years of disappointing Gillilands, these Red Havens were a dizzying, near-holy experience. (Note: when you spot the flatbed Gilliland truck, driven up from Cleveland, Tennessee, near the border, set up unannounced in a parking lot, you immediately stop and join the line, your previous agenda suddenly moot. The old-timer inspects the fruit in the basket he selected for you, replaces one or two, then yanks an inches-thick fold of bills from his overalls to peel off your change. These peaches have brought us twenty years of head-shaking, sticky-grinned pleasure, so I'm forgiving of recent history.)

Tomorrow at the Saturday market, there will still be some good late-season freestones, also the last of the crisp ears of white corn purchased by the dozen. Pints of blueberries. Honey, both wild-flower and sourwood. Tomatoes are at their best—those yellow grape tomatoes Claudia loves are sugar bombs in the mouth—as are the heavy, seedless watermelons, so dark they're almost black. Zucchini and cucumbers and summer onions in abundance, and eggplant shiny in rich purple skins. For the past two weeks, the surprise of local chanterelles, which we've eaten sautéed in garlic and olive oil and also, as we learned in the Dordogne, in simple omelets. I'll trade in my Mason jar for another unpasteurized half gallon from the Milk Lady, "for pet use only," and won't bother to wait. The beaded glass, the cold milk layered with cream, the first deep drink right from the bottle. Good lord.

As summer passes, there will be the compensation of apples, squash, pumpkins, pressed cider, finally even cooler days. No profound insights, just appreciating what remains as its brief moment intersects the fleeting moment we're alive to enjoy it. The abundance of the mistreated earth, those who still tend it, our community gathered and nourished. This isn't agrarian hogwash; it's common sense. How else would one behave?

Call of the White One

Today, we are told, is the birthday of Julius Caesar, Neruda, and Thoreau, and Chaucer was appointed as Chief Clerk to the King's Work in Westminster. So I am sitting thinking circularly of: a) betrayal by those you most trust; b) songs of love and despair; c) sucking out the marrow of life, preferably in the woods; and d) various self-serving and comical pilgrimages. In other words, it's all about me. But that group would be a lot of testosterone and a raucous dinner party.

Such whimsical thoughts, however, and what music and menu such an evening might include, are interrupted when dog Lucy decides enough's enough of keypad, screen, and my misconceived inattention to all things that matter. She is normally tolerant, lying perhaps between wall and reading chair with only an occasional sigh to note her displeasure. Or angled in the hallway so as to maintain vigilance of the entire house in case of sudden activity or clandestine snacking. Always, there is the distraction of the open front door, a wary eye out for any UPS delivery man with the temerity to turn down our drive. Sure, sometimes there's a scratching of the couch in mild frustration or the half-hearted taunt of a rawhide cigar, but generally she remains, if not understanding of, anyway resigned to these lost hours I hunch over the table.

Until, as I mentioned, enough's enough, some tipping point occurs indiscernible to human perception, and Lucy comes at me with a purposeful stride. She drives her head behind my knees, plush whiteness twisting beneath me, snout and diabolical smile emerging again, the entire toothsome beast of fur and claw turning in rebuke. She drops a smoked beef cheek at my slippered feet, and the gauntlet is thrown. *Bub, you think you're still alpha material? Bring it.* So much for impassioned sonnets, for living deliberately, for a lucrative sponsorship, for a night of wine and merriment with my pals. Just like that, the day's writing is abandoned. I'm onto my knees with a growl, splashing into the Rubicon, and the battle begins.

Blackberries

My father, into his eighties, surprised me with a half-full gallon bag of blackberries he'd picked at a secret location. As I recall, he lacked the resolve to can them as jelly or preserves, instead saving the entire stash as a gift for his youngest son. He had gone picking out of tradition and, I suppose, as an assertion of personal agency. What the hell.

Improbable as it seems, I'd guess that was five years ago. I got up this morning thinking guiltily of an icy Ziploc somewhere in the back of the freezer. That's a bad habit of mine, holding onto things too long, until they're ruined. These days, Dad can barely navigate their modest house, get to the grocer and back without incident, and those are the last blackberries he will ever pick. No crime in a bit of sentimentality, but certainly a misdemeanor to waste a batch of sweet wild berries.

But, as I dug through the overloaded shelves, they weren't to be found. I searched again, a bit frantically. No. I stood there, freezer door open, tendrils of cold on my face, a late-summer day already boiling outside. Perplexed, frustrated, resolve stolen. I looked a third time. At some point I'd felt similarly to this morning and made a cobbler or cooked down and strained a sauce for grilling. Maybe an ice cream. That's my theory, and a good thing, I suppose.

I share my father's nostalgia for berry picking. Sweat burning the eyes, shirt clinging, a barbaric August sun, every step into weeds potential snake pit awakened, chigger welts to be tallied later as wounds of honor across chest, stomach, and groin, torn hands and forearms streaked in blood, each plump, dark fruit revealed, taken, and added to the pail. Good country fun. The couple of small patches I discovered when I moved to Tennessee have long since been uprooted for subdivisions. I wouldn't know where to look.

As I said, there will be no more blackberries from my father. And
the last bag's gone.

Medical Center Plaza

Catching up on worn issues of *Good Housekeeping* and *Healthy Eating* to a droning backdrop of HGTV—hour after hour of dreams restored, visions fulfilled (or supplied), all with a wry joke and just within budget. This isn't my first vigil, recently, in the waiting room. Sour taste of Styrofoam coffee, sour taste of the future. My companions wait within their own stories, alone or in silent couples. A palpable sense of resignation, of inevitability. A vague perplexity we share. A tiredness. In my satchel—an unfinished book on French history that I've lost interest in, untasted fruits and candies, signed and unread miscellaneous paperwork, ancient Tracfone in case someone needs to be called. (Who's to be contacted, why, or to what purpose, I've no idea, but this is where we've arrived: a general, overriding caution, a habit of readiness for the inchoate worst scenario.)

In my shorts pocket, a state-of-the-art (to say *au courant* in this place would be gauche—France is a fiction now) buzzer, a glitzy apparatus, flickering blue, out of a sci-fi film. Its vibration will summon me once, twice, thrice to the far door to be escorted within for visit, update, or consult. Occasionally, the faint buzz of someone else bidden, a body getting up and trundling toward the door as it opens.

Don't get me wrong: Everyone here—all women, for some reason—is terrific. The receptionists; the general attendants; the anesthesiologists; the blonde surgeon who, except for her scrubs, looks like a cheerleader; Ashley in discharge who goes over the rules and warnings; the jocular Black woman who wheels the chair, at last, through the exit, are all terrific. Good-humored, knowledgeable, patient, kind, attentive. How lovely it would be never to see any of them again.

Have I mentioned I drive a 2004 Thunderbird, eggshell blue, limited edition with interior metal trim and white leather highlights? A flashy, preposterous ride that strangers my age or older, men and women alike, often admire when I am filling the tank. Low miles. Pristine body. Growling and unapologetic eight-cylinder engine. Fast, my friend, a relic of cool aplomb speeding through the continuum. *And yet*, you say, *not faster than destiny?*

For the moment, the rain has stopped, ceded to a suffocating humidity. The sky's not the glowing firmament of Provence, when it existed, but patches of sun have burned through. I lower the top, navigate the busy parking lot, turn the wheel, floor it toward the parkway and the new overpass beyond. The thick summer air mauls our hair, roughs our faces. *Who*, you ask, *may stem the tide of time?* as I get us the hell out of there.

Last Blooms

Picking daylilies doesn't elicit the guilt typical of cutting flowers. Maybe all that deadheading hardens one. Also, consider the sublime and the tragic: In addition to brief lives, the blooms are fragile, endearing them further to the poetic temperament. Think I'm joking? After a violent morning rain, step outside and inspect 130+ flowers of all styles and nuances, of perhaps thirty different varieties, gorgeous and luminous moments earlier and that you've waited a year for, ravaged to a mottled, goopy mess, their beauty taken. A gloomy sight.

Of course, it doesn't rain so much anymore. In the early evening I pick four flowers and float them in a glass bowl on the coffee table. I hold to the conceit that selection is prized by the plants, based on a hybrid's crazily productive day, a complementary palette of color, or personal whim. As the season wanes, a lily's final bloom—job well done—merits a wistful spot in the bowl. Always, though, I wait until early evening for my harvest, each flower deserving of its day in the sun, bold toward the sky or coquettish from within her foliage. Let the remaining bees have their fun, too, a good tumble in the pollen.

This game of hours can be risky. Yesterday afternoon, the very end of the season with two of only three remaining buds in bloom, a slashing gray storm arrived from nowhere. I was instinctively out of my chair and running, barefoot, onto the porch, down the slick stepping stones. No time for caution or jacket. Seconds could make the difference.

Happy ending: Our eccentric hero got to the lilies in time, snapped them from their stems. One in each hand and shielded by the body, he cradled his tender cargo, splashing through the grass back to safety. First responder!

That was yesterday. This morning, I tossed the remains, now a handful of goo, into the bin and scrubbed the bowl I would no longer need. The last bloom of the season, a rangy, golden Bengaleer—from when Virginia Peck liked tall scapes and lilies bold and up-faced, a style she later turned from for a more demure flower—hovers as lone sentry above the withered bed.

Which can only mean one thing: The hell of August is on its way. Time's up for ephemeral beauty. Time for the poets to lock their doors.

"At first, the man denied having sex with the horse."

Thus was the eye-popping pull quote from an article published one distant fall afternoon in the *Daily News Journal*, the local paper of Murfreesboro. I'd recently moved to town alone, loaded with stupid debt. I was driving a Plymouth Horizon my folks gave me—thank god—as a gift for completing my doctorate at Ohio State. From my apartment, I could walk the green space to a narrow stretch of the Stones River and stand in the debris and dog shit on its bank, watching the flow. Independence and adulthood at last. I'd taken a pay cut to an already laughable salary to escape Iowa and the feared "two-year college instructor" label.

I'd also given up writing fiction, especially novels, as a lost bet: There appeared no way around or through the specter of Hemingway. Papa, watching every move, shaking his craggy head, was too big for me. The poetry "career," meanwhile, felt stalled. I couldn't seem to beg, threaten, or cajole my way into a contract for a first book. I was writing reams of literary criticism (an illness it would take many more years to overcome).

As I recall the details of the article, a curious woman peeked through the hedge to find her sixty-eight-year-old neighbor naked and leading the horse into a carport, from where "unusual noises" began to be heard. I've forgotten the rest, but what further context could possibly be required? This was my new home. I blew up the quote and secured it to the filing cabinet in my campus office behind a "Rehab Is For Quitters" magnet, where they remained for many years, my odd personal mantras, until the tenor of the times prompted removal of both quote and magnet.

Well, I'd shafted them in Ottumwa, where they'd been kind to me and trusted me, but had gotten out unscathed after one year. I figured the Tennessee stint to be for three, give or take, then I'd make another leap. I'd grown up in the South and didn't intend to stay around long, especially not at a big state university. Surely, I was destined for some slick little MFA program, preferably on the beach, students waving the cooling fronds.

Commensurate with one's plans for life, next month I'll begin my twenty-seventh year at MTSU. I have an office with a window now. As to the equestrian amour of the sick old bastard in the newspaper? He would be well into his nineties, his riding days surely long over. He was fined $500. A lot of time has passed, and you'd hardly recognize Murfreesboro. Or me, I suppose.

Bill Morrissey

I'd spoken to Bill at the bar, before shows or during the break when he played in Nashville. He had a gloomy song about shooting his old dog that he knew upset me, so we'd joke about that, then typical of his humor he'd include it in the set. When his novel *Edson* came out, I invited him to campus to read. I think he enjoyed adding a literary gig to his tour schedule. (I'd reserved him a refurbished apartment in a dormitory, and he'd just arrived in the late afternoon and unwrapped a bottle of Jack Daniels after driving five hundred miles from Texas. About the third time we heard a hallway door slam, we decided he'd stay with us out at the house.)

So Bill Morrissey and I had agreeably crossed paths a few times, and I'm a huge admirer of his music, but we weren't friends. I hadn't seen him in years when my wife and I drove to an email-announced house concert an hour away. I was surprised when we entered the kitchen and the host said, without explanation, "Bill's on the porch." Indeed he was, sitting and tinkering with a guitar, and seemed delighted when we appeared. To describe him as gaunt is being kind. Afterward, I looked up his age. He was fifty-nine and could have passed for fifteen years older. Haggard and rail thin, but smiling, and still with that mischievous Morrissey glint in the eyes.

He died two days later, in a hotel room in Georgia. The house concert had an audience of eleven, including the hosts. Claudia requested "Birches," the closest thing to his signature song, and at the end of the night I called out for "Grave of Baudelaire." There's a recording, if you can find it, the last song of the last show, and, if they haven't cut the preamble, you'll hear Bill asking me to help him remember the lyrics.

Nocturne

The storm has cooled the night, and although I read today that the month just ended was the hottest in recorded human history, I sit quietly in pleasant darkness. Summers after they vanished, a few lightning bugs have returned to chart their positions. Not the blinking skies of my childhood, but numbers sufficient to encourage.

Perhaps I focus too much on losses—those arrived, those surely coming. Not to do so is a continual challenge. For many years I called out the clutches of baby screech owls from our woods. There was a precise shade of twilight that I came to know expertly, the tangible moment to hurry from the dinner table and begin my primitive trills at the edge of the clearing. They would arrive, swift and silent, often landing only feet above me. Keen, inquisitive, defining their merciless lives. We would do this dance every evening in summer and into autumn, until it was too dark for human eyes and I ceded to them their domain of night.

For a moment, the heat has relented. I listen to my breathing and let the dark settle into me. This wounded world, this immensity, to be a small part of it but belonging no less than any other. Somewhere behind, above the crickets and katydids, a tremulous, descending wail begins, a call I once attempted to learn. Ghostly hunter returned to say hello, or goodbye, or merely to gaze at what remains.

Famous Poet of the Midnight Sun

In the weeks leading up to my 2011 residency at the Arteles Creative Center in Finland, the director sent an email wanting to know if I'd agree to give a speech at the village's Midnight Sun Festival—lauding the beauty of the nights and so forth—casually mentioning that my "salary" would be in moose meat and vodka. I promptly accepted.

Rural Finland was greatly to my liking, but, as I devoted days to bicycling the vast countryside, swimming the lake as dragonflies circled my head, reading in the afternoons on a rickety porch laden with late-blooming hydrangeas, and being tortured naked in the center's sauna at ungodly hours of night, little signs and portents, the occasional referencing comment began to make clear to me the commitment was no joke. When I was informed that the Haukijärvi mayor and town council would like to see an advance copy of the speech the following week, my troubles were manifest. On the morning of the appointed day, I typed something up and in the afternoon was driven to a long, low wooden building that might once have been a schoolhouse but now served as part municipal locus, part museum of geological history. We had coffee, and someone had baked a cake. My two feeble pages were read, discussed, and approved without suggested revision or apparent enthusiasm.

The night of the festival arrived. Jocular and eccentrically decked out, we piled into two cars. I loosened my nerves with vodka shots. Finally, before a crowd of perhaps 150, I read out the words, pausing after each sentence for my lovely and raven-haired translator, Inga, to make sense of it. After opening remarks of appreciation for being invited, I broke the ice with a joke, warning of the suspicious behavior of my fellow artists and gesturing toward them. I stopped. Inga spoke. From the audience, silence. Having correctly surmised that my famous droll persona might not survive translation, I moved on to the meat of my message: the miracle of the evening, the vagary of the seasons, then with a flourish entreated us all to live gratefully and to celebrate the light, as the darkness always returns. Cornball.

The locals didn't swell into a chorus of delight, but neither did they toss me onto the pyre. Polite applause. I was presented with a pint of vodka—Finnish, of course—and a crock bowl of moose stew with dark bread. Not the haunch of animal I'd secretly hoped to carry off across my shoulders, but rich and warm and tasty. I ventured to eat "ceremoniously" for anyone who cared to watch. Then it was over. I rejoined my new friends for bad tango, more vodka, and laughter. An enormous bonfire reached into the gray but glowing sky of a night that wouldn't last forever.

Arthur Smith's Audience of One

At Art's memorial service that January in Knoxville, I reminisced about him once getting me into Tiger Haven for a tour. Among that afternoon's excitements, a lioness licked the top of my head. Tough to beat. I then read a poem of his that I published in *Poems & Plays* a dozen years earlier about the rare clouded leopard. "What an immense silence they make. / You don't notice it at first."

Considering the matter now, I realize that most of my stories involving Art also include wildlife. There was the enormous raccoon cage that filled his dining room. And a funny, revealing moment the last time I saw him vis-à-vis his relationship with his beloved Keeshonden, a rampaging trinity of dogs, who in latter years pretty much ruled the house.

But what I perhaps should have recounted at the service didn't involve animals or me, except as a gawking listener. Art said he'd once been invited to read at a music and literature festival and ended up scheduled opposite a popular singer, a headliner of the event. As a result, no one came to his reading. No one. An empty auditorium. This in itself constitutes merely a routine tale in the exalted life of the poet. The astounding part, however—and he not only swore to me it was true, but related it nonchalantly—was that he read anyway. To vacant seats. To. Vacant. Seats.

If anyone else had told me this, my Bullshit Detector would have been clanging away, and even so I was incredulous. "Hey guy," he offered as his matter-of-fact defense, "I had a contract." At one point, he further explained, a security guard came in and sat and listened to a couple of poems. It wasn't so bad.

Farewell, pal. The memorial was packed. I even wore a necktie—for a little while. Thanks for the lioness.

Being Kinky

Okay, here's one, I suppose, that's on me. The year 2006, and the Association of Writers & Writing Programs Conference riding roughshod over Austin. The AWP was still fun then but already beginning to metamorphose into the sprawling, impersonal, self-important mess it became. On the other hand—full disclosure—the Austin meeting also fell within a range of years during which the weekend's events were always rather hazy to me, so don't take my word for anything. But I can relay honestly that I've no idea, and never did, why I was asked to replace Kinky Friedman. (I do have a thought what power broker might have originated this dodgy and improbable suggestion, but I'll refrain from naming her.)

At the time, of course, Kinky was on the trail running for governor. He couldn't attend the session. (I know him well enough to say with confidence he'd never have set boot at such an event in any case. I don't know why he agreed to it.) So, flattered and vain and hungover, I said yes. Seemed like a good idea. Where the story goes from here is obvious, unrelated to whatever gibberish I'd scrawled in preparation for my place on the panel "Literary Citizens." It was a nice crowd, say three or four hundred. Cut to the priceless moment when I am announced as Kinky Friedman's replacement. A long beat. Then imagine half or more of the audience, as if on cue, collectively rising to head for the exits. I didn't blame them.

Later, I called the Kinkster from my room to relay the story and wish him well with his campaign. I remember telling him, for some unexpected reason, that I was proud of him. He really did sound harried, and it was a short conversation. Through the window from a high floor in the Hilton, I could see a dark cloud of the famous bats emerging from beneath the Congress Avenue Bridge, their numbers at the time estimated at 1.5 million. Kinky would collect more than half a million votes in the Texas gubernatorial election. I made a martini—a large one—as best I could with hotel provisions (no shaker, no olives). Soon, I'd go down to the bar to embrace my many friends and devotees. The night beckoned. Austin was a lively city. We would descend upon it. As I said, those days were a lot of fun—or something.

Blood Loaf: Ghoulish Limit of Culinary Taste? Hell No!

3 cups blood (duck, rabbit, pig, or . . .)*
1 cup stone-ground coarse white corn grits/polenta**
1 tsp. foie gras rendered fat***
1 large white onion
5 large cloves garlic
5–6 nice spears fresh marjoram or oregano (a loose ½ cup chopped)
½ tsp. allspice
½ tsp. freshly ground nutmeg
½ tsp. sea salt
12–15 grinds black pepper
6 oz. pork belly (skinned)****

Today is Charles Bukowski's ninety-ninth birthday, a humid and oppressive Sunday in August, and I am back in the kitchen laboratory I'd sworn closed forever following the completion of my cookbook-memoir *The Poet's Guide to Food, Drink, & Desire*.

And, of course, I am making a blood loaf.

The culprits for having me again raise the Henckels blade and don the mitt are a) an invitation by the editor of *Negative Capability* to embarrass myself and disgust the reader with an essay on said "loaf," offered as a coda of sorts to my recent book, and b) the opportunity to eliminate a half dozen small glass jars of duck and rabbit blood rather gruesomely accumulated in the freezer for the past year. Throughout *The Poet's Guide*, I mention and lament recipes that for various reasons—too esoteric, too complicated, too similar—didn't make the cut, and the "Afterword" is a résumé of these dishes (written as a parody of the final paragraphs of Hemingway's *Death in the Afternoon*, in case no one noticed). The blood loaf is *not* to be found among these excisions, lamented or otherwise, but I can't help giving it a whirl. The result, I speculate, will be cousin to a blood pudding—I dedicate an entire chapter to my adoration of the latter, "Blood Sausage and the Rudiments of Love"—without the casing and perhaps to the delicious goetta (pronounced "get-uh"). (Goetta is a German inspiration, packaged like rolls of sausage, made from pork and beef scraps, steel-cut oats, pork hearts and skin, onion, and spices. I recently came upon a few discounted pounds of Glier's and cannot stop eating the stuff sliced and browned in a skillet. Reportedly, and curiously, ninety-nine percent of all goetta produced is eaten in the greater Cincinnati/Northern Kentucky area.)

You're right, I'm stalling. Our bowl of blood awaits. (First, a necessary and long-winded detour on ingredients and asterisks. In the spirit of the fevered authority and discursive style of *The Poet's Guide*, I'm demanding here about ingredients but then try to step back and be reasonable. "Is Brewer really serious about this stuff," the reader may wonder, "or is it just part of his attempt at cheeky fun?" Yes.

(Okay, let's knock out all of the asterisks in one fell swoop and then get on with our dubious culinary endeavor. *I saved duck and rabbit blood from animals thawed and butchered over the past year or so, so that's what I'm using. No run-of-the-mill blood loaf for me! That's the joke, and I'll stand by it, although I imagine pork blood would work as well or better here, fresh if you can get it. Since two toney butcher shops I know carped [when I chastised them about not making in-house blood sausage] that regulations are so stringent that they can't use the blood, we're probably talking about going straight to a farmer or, say, local at-home sausage maker. Ask around about the blood. Maybe somebody "knows a guy." Of course, be evasive and mysterious re its purpose. By the way, my little jars yielded three cups, so that's our arbitrary measurement for the recipe.

(**I drone on quite tediously in *The Poet's Guide* about local sourcing, with one special advocacy being milled flour and meals. We give our custom to two nearby Tennessee mills. If you want to grab a bag of yellow corn grits off the shelf of Kroger, even for such a noble enterprise as this, it'll do.

(***I happened to have a small container of fat saved from slices of foie gras I seared, the former an ethereal substance appropriate for nearly any purpose, food-related or otherwise, which also complemented the loaf's vague "duck" theme. Bacon fat's fine as an alternative.

(****I came across some beautiful fresh pork belly, so I used it. Back fat, a solid piece of jowl bacon, or, in a pinch, any thick-cut bacon should suffice.

(Lastly, a note on the "comely but unadventurous food companion" who appears throughout *The Poet's Guide* and claims she got a bad rap. Vis-à-vis blood loaf, it should go without saying that you'll be alone on this one, abandoned in the kitchen and possibly the house. Well, at least you'll claim a few faint accolades for getting those morbid jars out of the freezer.)

Enough with the niceties. Let's cook blood.

In a large skillet, melt the foie gras fat and sauté your finely chopped onion on a medium-low burner for three minutes. Don't let it brown. Add the finely chopped garlic for three more minutes, stirring occasionally with a spatula until the onion is translucent. Add the allspice, the ground nutmeg, the salt, the ground pepper, the chopped marjoram or oregano, the blood, and the grits, and stir together.

Turn burner up to medium and cook for five to six minutes, stirring now and then, until the mixture thickens. If you've the fortitude, taste for seasoning, but it should be about right. In a smaller, separate skillet, sauté the coarsely chopped pork belly for three to four minutes, until half-cooked, and stir into the other ingredients.

Spray a loaf pan (I used a glass model by Pyrex) with vegetable oil, pour in the blood mixture, cover with aluminum foil, place in a larger baking dish, and gently fill the larger dish with boiling water. Bake at 350°F for eighty to ninety minutes or until firm. Take a look now and then. If you've some liquid on and around the loaf after, say, an hour, you might remove the aluminum foil.

Lift from the water bath and cool in the refrigerator. Have another martini. Go to bed.

The next morning, when you invert the loaf on a cutting board, yes, its ashen shade may be disheartening. Yes, it may be leaking a discolored and disquieting fluid. (Perhaps the result of water in the thawed blood?) And yes, the texture is off-putting and the consistency infirm, a slice disintegrating against the blade into a crumbled mess. This was never a project for the weak-willed or spiritually discouraged. Anyway, "the proof is in the blood loaf," no?

Brown a slab in a small skillet with a bit of butter. The taste, I believe you will surprisingly concur, is agreeable—the spice and corn flavors pleasant and up-front—although admittedly that gray mush isn't much to look at. Brown a second small test batch, this time scrambling it with a beaten farm egg. The dreary appearance remains unimproved, but see if the result isn't even tastier, with an unusual profile of savory flavors and a curious texture in the mouth. Be honest: It's good, maybe even very good, even if you're just a bit disappointed to have marginally avoided total humiliation and utter failure. There's always next time.

The second iteration above reminds me greatly of the scrambled pork brains and eggs my folks sometimes made when I was a kid. I remember the gray mound in the bowl, a taste peculiar but edible. This scrambled egg and blood loaf, though, is downright yummy. You may even find that you'd be willing to sit down and eat more. By *choice*. If this endorsement doesn't send you scurrying to source a quart of fresh animal blood, I don't know what will. Enjoy.

The loaf will last several days in the refrigerator before you throw away the remains and would probably freeze well, if you're willing, that is, to again preserve the blood and continue the gory cycle. My recommendation: eat a bit yourself—again, you'll likely be alone except for the dog—to prove your inchoate point, then mush some into small sealed containers and "gift" to family, friends, enemies, and your department chair.

Hm. Well. That's that, and our quest continues. Perhaps we'd have been wiser ordering blood sausages from La Tienda, my go-to online company for all comestibles Spanish, and picking up a few pounds of goetta the next time we're driving from Louisville to Columbus. I've been experimenting with a seductive cardamom ice cream, the green pods roasted and crushed, then steeped in the batter's hot milk and cream. Sexy. Maybe we should have gone that way . . .

And, de rigueur: *bon appétit*.

Coming Home from the Georgia Coast, Late Summer

Sunday, a day early, but those murderous temperatures, and we'd had our gators if not our dolphins, our tidal marsh kayak if not our sunset river cruise, decent meals if never a feast, and we missed that damned dog. So, early fugitives from the Airbnb, pushing hell-bent for nine hours and feeling every one of them and every year of fifty-plus in ass and back, neck, shoulders, we turn into the gravel drive, a dappled tunnel of overhang. At the end of it, the house still stands! I wheel the car around to face outward, and we climb stiffly out. There's Kellum, aspiring young poet, just off shift at the garden shop, watering the flowers. He waves as we waste no time unloading. Heavy bags for me, the rest of the jumble as one can grab, hauled as quickly as possible across the jungle of the yard, door unbolted and everything inside. The front porch I refinished before we left, though littered with leaves, shines amber and glossy in the late afternoon. The house is a furnace. Crank down the thermostat in the front, crank it down in the back. Make it all a freezer for the girl. Then unspoken divisions of labor: Claudia to pay the kid, finish the "thank you"s for keeping everything alive, and back in the Subaru off to collect Lucy, whom we've been informed from the road is freshly bathed, newly trimmed, and, we are confident, smelling good! Gaylord to grab the keys to his T-Bird and gun it—but top up, baby—to the grocer for provisions of roasted chicken, slaw, biscuits, juice, something sweet. At the rendezvous, I am moments behind them. My girl scratching the storm door, frantic as I pull in, coming at a lope despite the heat. And no kidding: in the interim forty minutes, the moonflower on the porch has unfolded a single, billowing kerchief to welcome us home. The crimson hibiscus heavy with buds will open tomorrow, blooms wider than my spread hand. But that's tomorrow.

The Beemer and the Doe

I heard the impact from one hundred yards. By the time I'd jogged to the end of Primrose Lane, the tableau of carnage was determined. Her position, fifty feet behind, on the grassy berm opposite, head lying toward the street, made no sense to me. Had she tried to run, and spun as she collapsed? The delicate legs shattered beneath her, their unnatural angles hard to witness. She looked at me, panting hard, tongue thick in her mouth. I knelt and stroked the beautiful, muscled neck, whispered what I could. My heart hammering. No way to end her pain.

The driver leaned on the fender in his pressed slacks, open shirt collar, unseasonal tan and swoop of sandy hair. Ray-Bans. Barking inconvenience into his phone, he never once looked back. I approached the BMW—a 330i sedan, Mediterranean blue, polished to a shine—and took what pleasure I could from its mangled grill, shattered headlight. This man was, of course, my enemy. I recognized him, hated him, wished him harm.

I hiked on as planned, east along Highway 96. Late afternoon. The day shimmering, palpable. It was no good. I felt dizzy. Overwhelmed with anger. I turned and walked back, past the car, past the man still animate with self-concern, back to where she lay. A pool of foam around the parted lips. The green eye a glassy marble. The chest still. The mercy of death, and no need for useless sympathy. That wild beauty gone from the earth.

The Marshall House

On a sweltering August afternoon when only a man deranged would return to Savannah, I wheel up to the stately brick facade and green shutters and park the car in valet like I own the place. Today, I toss the key to Teyron, adjust my Panama hat, and watch him load the luggage cart. It's his birthday, and he is "spectacular." Calhoun holds open the hotel door and, in a bulging-eyed bit of schtick, calls out "*Ahh*, y'all's come back to visit us old folks *again*!!" The cold lobby, with its tiled pineapple of welcome, is the world restored. At reception, Allysia—who called last week to ask in what special way she might prepare for our arrival—smiles wide. The Mary Marshall Suite is ready for early check-in.

Ah, the Mary Marshall Suite. It twelve-foot ceilings and crown moldings, the scarred and polished wide-board floors, the claw-foot tub soon to be put to use. I pause in the hallway on a padded scarlet and purple runner that stretches to eternity. Under the dandyish eye of a triple-matted rendering of the good governor, James Edward Oglethorpe, I open the door. In the suite's sitting room, a surprise bottle of brut champagne on ice, a welcome back note signed by the staff. Teyron arrives with the luggage. I guess he's twenty-three. He's beaming. He's thirty-one. I shove a handful of bills at him. Happy birthday, my man. Deep pockets are essential. Tip the bellhop, tip the valet who collects the car, tip the maid for her kind service, tip the girl who brings me coffee and a pitcher of cream in the atrium in the morning. Tip the Lord for that which He bestoweth. At the Marshall House, I am a generous man.

Yes, we could speak of the building's 1851 construction, of its months in 1865 as a military hospital, of its ghostly overtures. (Conrad Aiken? Johnny Mercer? The Union dead?) But I commend the present. Much to do. After unpacking, there's the afore-mentioned bath in aforementioned clawfoot tub, with restorative mineral salts after an arduous trip. Then stepping through the long window onto the veranda overlooking Broughton Street. A flute of the bubbly, the first chapter of a new mystery mailed to the hotel and awaiting me at the desk. Tatted-up SCAD students pass beneath, full of the future. Tourists in baggy shorts, meandering with to-go cups, point up at the handsome ironwork, the slow-turning fans, the distinguished man in a rocking chair, sipping champagne. Someone takes a photograph.

But time is short. The evening wine reception is beginning in the library, a harp concert by the ravishing Kristin King. Afterward, dinner reservations and a late stroll home through a few of the quarter's more romantic squares.

In Chattanooga, the Old Fort Inn is gone.

In Birmingham, the Pickwick Hotel is gone.

Outside Asheville, the Sourwood Inn has recently been sold by the family.

At time of writing, the Marshall House remains. God bless it.

Origin Story, Lucy

They played me like a fiddle, all right. I see that now. Cedaridge Collie Rescue. Wicked, wicked people. On the way to visiting my folks outside of Louisville, I had the laughable misjudgment to make a detour to inspect—just for the fun of it, mind you, no commitment—an abandoned litter of American Eskimo puppies I'd seen advertised online. When I pulled up to the house, collies surrounded the Chrysler in a raucous maneuver. I was surrounded. I levered the door open, eased out, made it onto the porch alive. Already, matters were out of control.

Diane tipped the laundry basket and five white balls of fluff, still damp from their baths—she had washed them just for me—rolled onto the spread blanket. They were on me immediately, all female, four plump Kentucky girls and one tiny one. I'd noticed the latter in the website photos, barely edging into the frames: a single eye, a bit of chin, a fragment of drooped ear amidst her effusive sisters. For act two, Diane opened a door to the garage and their mother Rose entered at a sprint. She was pretty, looked tired, and immediately lay on her side, resigned to the pandemonium. Each of the big girls chose a teat and happily went at it. The little one sat back on her hind legs, teatless, looking around vaguely. The heart-rending holiday story: all found deserted in the backyard of an empty house, father taken by animal control . . . I stood and, managing not to step on anyone, hurried from the house, negotiated the collie posse, and escaped.

The weekend with my parents was festive and enjoyable, but I felt increasingly distracted, indefinably nervous. It was December in the weeks before Christmas. Finally, I confessed to them what was up, confessed to the simple fact that I had, apparently, lost my mind. I called Cedaridge and Diane, the Devil incarnate, answered.

"Uh, hi, this is, um . . . I mean, hey, I was there on Friday, looking at those, um, Eskimo pups? Anyway, I was just wondering, I don't know, if that small one was still, you know, available, probably not, I guess, huh?"

"The runt? Sure. We've been saving her for you."

Next morning, Mom folded a small Humane Society blanket into a shoebox, and I left a day early, fool for love.

Origin Story, Lucy, Part II: The Introduction

Lucy—I'd tried out the name as we drove and liked it—was eight weeks old, the runt of the litter, a cottony fur-ball that fit comfortably in the palm of my hand. Her blanketed shoebox on the passenger floorboard was commodious, and she slept soundly during the three hours toward her new home. Meanwhile, my heart thrummed with its devious secret.

Twenty miles out, we stopped at a square of green beside a Publix grocery, and I lifted her onto the grass. She wobbled around, oozing liquidy poop from spot to spot. Adorable! (I'd forgotten the puppy skillset. That night, as she carpet-bombed our bedroom carpet a dozen times, it began to occur to me that I perhaps hadn't fully planned out the adoption transition process.)

At last, I turned into the drive, pulled into the garage, and began to unpack from my trip, leaving the mutt dozing again in Reebok splendor. The December afternoon was cool and pleasant, so no problem. At this point, I must mention that I have a reputation—utterly unfounded—of being surly and judgmental when I return from a trip. Trash in the street, a yard full of sticks, mud on the porch, a greasy stovetop—any of these might sour my happy homecoming, goes the preposterous and defaming myth which I now planned to use to my advantage.

Claudia was in her study at the computer. I said hello, gave her a kiss, and spent an excruciating ten to fifteen minutes putting away toiletries, filling the hamper with dirty clothes, plugging in the holiday lights, *inter alia*. That is, relishing my deception. Each minute I waited further sweetened the payoff.

Finally, I couldn't stand it. I crept back to the car and, cradling the box behind me away from the house's windows, stomped back in the front door.

I took a breath, then called out in my most exasperated voice: "Claudia, what is *this*?" My reading chair askew? Dust on the lampshade? The carpet pile not uniformly combed? I shifted my accent. "*What* is this?"

Even from down the hall, I heard the tired trepidation in her voice. "I'm coming."

Thrice, for good measure: "What *is* this?"

My wife came around the corner, saw me standing there, grinning stupidly beside the coat hooks hung with candy canes and bells, nutcrackers and blinking lights.

She stopped. Her mouth opened but no words came out. I handed her the shoebox, and Lucy is what it was.

"Something there is that doesn't love a wall."

How not to relive it, the only unprotected periphery of our land, and the two decades we were lucky, until we weren't, and denied the chance to purchase the vulnerable frontage, and the conniving son of a bitch who cleared it all, the bulldozer every day for a week, the cracking of hackberry and elm and ash and oak ripped by the roots, and I a witness each hour of each day of that hell, helpless as they razed what we had protected and nurtured, the incessant breaking of the trunks like screams until I thought I'd go mad, and dreaming blood, and my wife arriving home at the end and, seeing the destruction, dropping her satchel, falling to her knees and crying out against what was lost and not to be restored, our old lives gone, and in the months that followed the sad defense, too late, of 440 feet of cedar planking, eight feet tall, full privacy fencing for privacy lost, the irony of the trees of our own felled for a clear line, and what that wall finally cost us, what it finally cost me.

A year has passed. Behind the fence, the cracked earth of the clearing remains. The violence of that carnage still stuns. The goddamned insolence. We still own forested acres to the east and the northwest of the house, but without the contiguous passage of cover animals require—and what, anyway, can surmount an eight-foot fence?—we no longer see deer that were commonplace, that we knew by name. Our past catalog of visitors: red and gray fox, coyote, bobcat, wild boar, possum and coon and rafters of turkey in abundance. All gone. Or, a better thought, perhaps out of sight, biding and cautious. Sitting last night in the muggy August twilight, I watched a single, wide-eyed rabbit—wary but hungry for the grass—as it watched me. And in the last light, a flash of armor, armadillo briskly across the gravel drive back into undergrowth. Armadillo have only migrated here in recent years. We welcome them, as we do the black bear now sometimes caught on camera as near as two counties away, always a single young male exploring the boundaries, seeking a home range of his own. I fear for the ignorance, the savagery those beautiful bears will encounter.

We didn't want a fence for our good neighbor. We wanted wildness.

Still Not Illegal, Not Yet a Sin

To sit alone, silently, listening to percussive thunder, the steady applause of a rare August rain, the coursing gutter spouts, the squeak of an unseen hummingbird somewhere out in the cooling assault. To sit on the swing in the easy, meditative motion of your own thoughts, or of no thoughts at all, while reverence is still allowed without interference of law. To inhale the greening of the grass, the bloomed-out crepe myrtle bowed beneath the storm's reprieve. That is, to remain. The bounty of the darkened sky, curtain drawn over a day prematurely ended. Don't tell me the world doesn't sigh in collective relief, in a shared and wondrous sadness of memory. Don't tell me I shouldn't think so, or feel as I do.

First Day of School, 1971

A world of black and white, iterations of gray, just a shade out of focus. Poured into a T-shirt, hands on hips as if braced for the inevitable, a single scrawny tree for company. What speaks more than anything is the child's grim countenance. The narrowed eyes, the mouth unsmiling in a fleshy face. Some unpleasant shit is about to come down. In a moment, he will step into the harrowing hallways of John J. Audubon Elementary. Parked behind him four vintage autos—long, angular sedans. He doesn't notice or care. Olds 98? Chevy Impala? This is no time for distraction. He senses that life is about to suck, and keep sucking. But he's ready. How appropriate that the frame cuts him off at the knees.

My father insisted on our education but found cruel amusement in the Sunday dinner before school started each fall—oh ominous day—when he'd remind his youngest, for example, "Well, only nine more years to go!" or perhaps, "Son, just eight more years!" then tuck back into his pork and gravy. And that was only high school. Him having a GED furthermore made college nonnegotiable, so add four more years to the bad news. A lifetime. Conversely, my older brothers and I never attended preschool, kindergarten, or the like. Mom and Dad wanted their boys at home. (Matters for me were ultimately even worse. Tack on graduate school, and, to escalate it all to absurdity, nearly three decades of teaching. You've surmised correctly: I write these words on the last Sunday in August. Summer is over, the fall semester begins tomorrow. That sinking feeling remains.)

The photograph's amusing, wistful and, yes, prophetic. My mother took it after escorting me to my doom that morning. I think I recall a portion of the journey, as the sidewalk curved and we came within view of the low brick building, but the memory may be fanciful. Beyond the border of the picture, now I see her, holding a cheap camera, memorializing her baby's big day. By my math she's thirty-five. Young and pretty. The year before, my folks had taken a leap of financial faith and moved us into their dream home, meaning where we'd stay beyond the standard two to three years, where they'd finish raising their boys. The next dozen years will be the happiest of their lives. Excuse my presumption, but I believe so.

Back to our disquieting subject. The kid looks like he's maybe holding his breath. Chubby fingers grip belt loops. No more stalling. Time to turn around, enter those doors. Will it be as bad as he anticipates? Probably. He'll attend Audubon Elementary for two grades. The year after, the school will be ravaged by the Great Tornado of 1974. Missing roof, desks hanging in shattered trees, all the optics. But a tornado is neither symbol nor will of God. And it has nothing to do with this story. Off we go, lad.

Hollywood, Here I (Don't) Come!

I'll never verify whether the Chesterfield Film Company had a policy of sadism, but their notification protocol enjoyed a perversity that held one's attention. I'm going to guess the year as 1990, maybe 1991, and I was in the stretch run of a PhD at Ohio State, probably ABD. On a lark, I submitted some short plays to Chesterfield's Writer's Film Project. Twenty fellows would be given a stipend to cover living expenses for a yearlong workshop. The program was under the auspices of Spielberg's Amblin Entertainment, and participants were virtually assured leisure sunbleached afternoons with Francis out at the vineyard, egg-white omelet brunches with sycophantic William Morris agents, a foothold in the industry. Hoo-wah. As I remember the literature, I am being only mildly facetious.

I received a call from a Chesterfield representative informing me that my submission had been one of seventy selected from an international pool of 1,200 applicants. I was a semifinalist for the fellowship. They'd be in touch. Claudia and dog Jasper and I had recently committed to moving in together, in a fairly nice townhouse apartment several miles from campus. The call was amusing, deserving of a toast and some imaginative indulgence.

Several weeks later, the phone rang again. I was now one of twenty, a finalist for the ten fellowships. More soon. They'd be in touch. This revised news was less amusing. I now had a one in two chance of receiving the damned thing. Toss of a friendly coin. Most disturbing was that I knew in my heart that if I won, I'd go. How could I not? Leave the degree incomplete, blow up my new life, move to Hollywood alone for a year that would certainly, unforeseeably, irrevocably change my future. How could it not?

More weeks passed. I tried to stay cool and get on with the pleasant new rituals of simulated adulthood. Then the phone rang again. And no kidding, I swear what follows is the truth. The ten fellowship recipients had been determined. I had been selected as number eleven, *the first alternate*, if anyone decided or otherwise needed to decline!

The rest of this story, or rather non-story, is self-evident, although I did indulge a kind of James Cain/Patricia Highsmith scenario of obtaining the list of ten and then, say, taking a nice, careful road trip to maybe Omaha or Kansas City, biding my time on a residential street, then smothering a stranger in his bed, some talentless chump getting what he deserved, the needed name crossed off. I've a general theory that the older one gets, the more settled into relationships, career, and your own skin, the more seismic the event required to profoundly alter the direction of a life. In my case, I can think of only two other comparable paths not taken. Hell, offered the fellowship now, I wouldn't even consider moving to LA to kiss ass and live like a pauper for a year. But I'm also no longer twenty-five, broke, or a student. For better or worse, the award would have changed everything. The Omaha murder might have made a good screenplay. Option for a sequel.

II: AUTUMN

*Charlton Heston's Bible; tornadoes then &
now; creamy polenta; lust in the heart; all of
human history; crown of thorn; book festival
malaise; trespass; hawk; open casket*

September 1st, Sunday, 12:18 p.m. . . .

. . . so the day now begins its contraction. Four months of the year remain, 121 dawns, one third of its possibilities. Coordinates. Afternoon will pass into evening, then those hours too vanish and one day more be removed from the sum. Mathematics. The solace of cooler days will arrive—not yet, but soon, what choice but patience?—and the late harvest of apples, figs, pumpkins, all varieties of squash. Bouquets of mum and aster. The balm of October. The lengthening nights, the soft fabrics, the slumber that follows. Incantations.

What else will the coming months bring? Lucy will turn eleven, cause for celebration and melancholy. She remains playful and often happy, with only a slight diminution of motion, a practical economy, as evidence of time. Our home is comfortable, our lives bounteous and secure, possibly beyond what can be trusted. We are educated and generous. Our health is good, manageable, and there is every reason for gratitude and awe, for to us the world has been given.

And yet. What is this foreboding, this heaviness of heart? This dark conviction advancing between the trees, even as the sky is bright, the future beckoning? This something that will not be vanquished or named. Forgive me. This was a day better offered to silence. But perhaps you sense it as well, and wait as I do.

Tomorrow Would Be a Long Day

Fiddling at the stove with my bachelor dinner, believing you'd already left, I was surprised by the single honk that brought me and dog Lucy to the door. We watched you pull away. Suddenly, choke of dust rising from beneath tires, my favorite cover of the Dylan song harmonious in the room, my throat contracted. I couldn't swallow, my breath was short, and I was overcome. The parched gravel drive, the car receding, receding, turning from view. You were gone. Although I knew the scene I watched was fantasy, I saw it no less vividly: you leaving us, hatchback askew with boxes and books, lamps and pillows, tears and anger at lives never to be put back together, the stupid waste of it all. I stood there, blinking, foolish, staring at the empty passage. How grateful was I that, instead, you were merely off to the city for the evening, a play in rehearsal, my dinner a one-off mess rather than a long horizon of lonely meals. I checked the burners, began the song again, and returned to bolt the door. Two young does ambled in the drive, sampling perimeter plants. We rarely see deer here anymore, but there they were—lovely, alive, curious, chastising my indulgence. In a few hours you'd be home. No separation, no collision. I'd probably be asleep, a little drunk. But outdoor lights to welcome you, the hot and sour soup you love in the fridge. Into your pajamas, hello, a bit of TV to unwind.

In the future, however distracted you are with thoughts of your script, the director, the inexperienced actors, my harshness, our rituals of disregard, you can kiss me goodbye twice any time you like. What a long day tomorrow would be, what a crooked trail, if otherwise.

Havel

The tragedy of modern man is not that he knows less and less about the meaning of his own life, but that it bothers him less and less.

—Václav Havel

I didn't plan it, hadn't even considered it, not my style. The closing night of *The Beggar's Opera* at Columbia, an incisive production with delightful cutouts and, if memory serves, life-size puppetry. Mr. Havel was in residence at the university and in attendance, front of the house.

The show was over and we were all standing, wrapping ourselves in winter gear—it was December—against the cold New York night. Suddenly, I had to meet him. I can't explain the impulse or its urgency, but I recall that as I started forward from the back of the theater—having said nothing to my wife or in-laws—I progressed easily through the tide of the departing crowd. I suppose Mr. Havel spotted my movement upstream and intuited its purpose, because when I looked up he was watching me.

The googled date, 2006. I'm amazed the year was so recent. Of course, Havel was still the Czech Republic president until 2003, just a blink of history ago. My god, it seems a lifetime since then. A different world now, much diminished, and thinner than ever on heroes.

I approached the man, muttered something inane. He grinned beneath a graying mustache. Then he offered me his hand, and I took it.

Charlton Heston's *The Holy Bible*

The late '90s, Louisville. I'd taken my mother out to lunch, dutiful son that I was and remain, and as a coincidental surprise we stopped at Hawley-Cooke Booksellers (long since defunct) where Heston was signing copies of his *Charlton Heston Presents the Bible*: the Scriptures' worthier stories redacted and revisited, with photos of the legend himself in various locales of the Holy Land. Khaki pants, denim work shirts with sleeves rolled above muscular forearms, confident and ready—he was there where it happened.

A long line of waiting readers snaked around the bookcases, entirely older women dressed to the nines. Who could blame them? Ben-Hur, Moses, El Cid, General Andrew Jackson. Quite possibly, the last man standing. Except the elderly actor was sitting, of course, in wool blazer and tie, surrounded by stacks of coffee-table volumes, and I watched fascinated as each devotee approached. Heston not only made eye contact beneath that famously bushy brow and offered that famously craggy smile, but laid a hand on each woman's wrist. A benediction. Of course, each wanted to be touched by him, and this he knew and accepted by rite.

The line crept along, its length slowly diminished. Listen: Charlton Heston may have been a gun-worshipping fascist, prone to gaffes, but that made him no less an iconic badass among cowering mortals. (I once attempted to write out the quotable lines from *The Ten Commandments*, a goal I soon gave up as pointless. It is the most beautifully bombastic film of all time, without argument. Nearly every line, from the mouths of both Moses and likewise *über*-badass Ramses II/Yule Brynner, is poster-worthy.) For my money, the middle-aged Heston, box-office rank slipping, was baddest of all. Within an astounding handful of years he gave us *The Omega Man*, *Soylent Green*, the malevolent Cardinal Richelieu. Need a life mantra? Look no further than the opening of *Planet of the Apes*, the gleefully snarling George Taylor: "You got what you wanted, tiger. How does it taste?"

Mom enjoyed seeing Heston, and we stood nearby a while. She had no interest in purchasing a Bible once she saw the price. They had Bibles at home. Fair enough. Still, looking back, I wish I'd been less self-conscious about waiting in the line, less concerned with seeming cool and detached. I, myself, could have received the Touch and walked out blinking into the brilliant clarity of afternoon, holding close a copy of The Holy Book, signed by the author.

Yellow Sky

By the time the sky is yellow, it is too late to hide, warns the folk wisdom. And this reckoning—amber hue across trees and lawn, golden glow of redwood fence—draws you out into the palette of a heightened world. The sky's conviction more placid than roiling, the cumulus sure and slow in congregation, the iridescent pathways. Witness, supplicant, dupe. Who may resist the assembling storm?

Today the hottest in recorded human history for this calendar date. The defeated garden, the fractured earth. All of this is appropriate, as are the last rains, relief so long past to seem myth, a wishful story we told ourselves. You knew when they came again they would come a gale force, beautiful and ravaging.

The first strike of lightning connecting sky to earth brings you joy. The second strike, horizontal from one charged cloud to another, is pure forgiveness. Together, these nails of fire form a cross meaning nothing. You raise the prism of your drink. In response, the hot wind, the shuddering oak and willow, the manic flight of leaf torn free.

Keep it simple. *Show me the magic*, you whisper, a private joke. If you still had your powers, you would happily cede them to the rousing tempest. The first fat drop of rain hits your face. Another splashes in the dust at your bare feet. What a comforting thought to soon be gone, aberrant and banished. Bear and wolf, the great sequoias, resuming. What a blessing to stand here in this sovereign last moment. What grace to be too late.

Shelter from the Storm

And more than shelter—creamy polenta with fresh gulf shrimp and homemade sauce made from the season's last tomatoes and basil. The dish is spectacularly delicious. Addictive, I confess. For added ambience to the howl and swirl beyond darkening windows, the glow of three votive candles nestled in the playful ceramic holders miraculously gotten home unbroken from a village shop in Provence. All the comfort and privilege one could want, or bear, and the moment flawed only by Lucy's absence. Her instinct for rough weather turns her odd and anxious long before we sense what's coming. Soon she's in the doorway, offering a forlorn last look over her shoulder, then under the bed for the duration, whence no call of promised safety will coax her.

I find impending storms irresistible and had taken up my typical position in the yard, challenging the wind, reading the sky for blades of lightning as trees around me bowed. A delighted conjurer minuscule in the immensity, invoking the gods' violence, desirous for their retribution. At the height of my incantation, the porch light blinked twice. Dinner was ready. I strove to continue the magic, a distracted taunt toward hastening clouds. The porch light blinked again, three times. Dinner was being plated. Now. Such the yin and yang of mortal destiny, a foot in each of two worlds. The storm wouldn't wait. Neither would the shrimp. Of course, I lowered my arms, turned from the thunder of the east, and entered my comfortable home. The candles were lit. The polenta was, as I mentioned, fabulous. By the time we emptied the bowls, the worst outside had passed, but it would be a while before Lucy, ever erring on the far side of caution, would rejoin us.

Friday the 13th, Harvest Moon

Risk no chances tonight. Instead, take from the box your sachet of salt scaled from human skin, your vial of water stoppered by the Last Holy Man. Take your tress of virgin hair, your amulet of bear claw and silver. Take the dance of the tallow candle. Commodities for night's passage. Listen: We are sophisticated folk, you and I, educated, aloof to the auguries of calendar and sky. But why court trouble in troubled times? Pascal's prudence.

Those shuffling footsteps, the late fist at the door, the ravening stranger? That is, hair risen on your neck and a lone dog embellishing the darkness with its pain? A rasping name that could be your own? Go ahead. Answer. Time was, you were the predator, so you fancied, and perhaps you may once more be dangerous.

In either case, one way to find out. The trembling curtain. The door flung wide.

Moonlight floods the room.

Trust me.

Talking to My Father

I call to ask after his swollen foot and ankle. No better. The un-surprising result, I am told matter-of-factly, of a botched surgery for clogged arteries. No further explanation offered or requested. Does the swelling go down as he limbers up during the day? No, it gets worse. It's not too bad in the morning. Anyway, fuck it, he's got comfortable slippers. His knees are the problem.

As we talk, I notice that he is lucid, engaged, and that he can actually hear me, mostly. He is obviously glad to be bullshitting with his youngest son and not in the usual hurry to hand me off. The old dark humor is there, an engagement beyond the enclosing walls of his pain. We joke a bit about the jolly subject of amputation, and he casually recalls that Emmitt lost his leg just before dying in Alaska, which I don't remember. Anyway. He put Emmitt down after what he did to Pirtle.

No, he's doing all right. To my knowledge, he hasn't fallen for sev-eral weeks. I don't ask. See, I have my dad back for a few minutes. He is recognizable, something like himself, and I am talking to him. We linger for a few more seconds. Anyway, he took Peyton to the park that afternoon and let him run. Almost never got the little bastard back in the Buick. Here's my mother. He'll try to stay alive until my next visit.

When I hang up, I am still smiling but feel a deep quiet that will last all evening. These difficult days the only remaining ones we will ever have.

Home Birding

What pleasure to refill the birdbath with clean cool water for the Robin's relief as heat marches unrelenting into autumn. The Cardinal too arrives thirsty, and the Blue Jay's screech is, I believe, appreciative. The feeder does steady business despite the squirrels' tireless scheming. A fine Red-Bellied Woodpecker has been a regular lately; his distinctive *chuck chuck* brings me to the window. Also of that family, we have the Downy, the occasional Flicker, rarely the unmistakable hammering in the woods of the grand Pileated at its work (and, once in twenty years, not one but a *pair* investigating the lawn!). Nearby, in a peculiar microclimate of a few hundred yards, and nowhere else, we've seen the rakish Red-Headed.

There's hardly space to catalog the chorus of my friends, the common abundance of Nuthatch and Sparrow, Chickadee, Titmouse, and Wren. The pensive coo of the Mourning Dove. And even now, sometimes a new arrival. Who's that inquisitive little fellow on the porch, looking in? Cerulean Warbler, according to my books. Welcome! At the tree line, rustling just out of sight among fallen leaves, I hear the Rufous-Sided Towhee. I love the migratory visits of the Indigo Bunting, iridescent, and the large and handsome Rose-Breasted Grosbeak (unfortunately, not seen for years). Perhaps once each winter a flock of Cedar Waxwing amid bare branches. The Ruby-Throated Hummingbird, meanwhile, departs the first week of October, as if on cue, suddenly and without farewells. I cheer when the Goldfinch—what my folks called a "Wild Canary" when I was a boy—takes on his glowing yellow plumage, announcing summer has arrived. The irregular visitor of the Brown-Headed Cowbird, the Mockingbird who prefers the suburbs, and, just as well, the bully Starling. A dozen years ago, a pair of elusive Crimson Tanager, male and female, that appeared after Jasper died and as I buried him between the hydrangeas beneath Claudia's window, the augury of their purring song I still associate with grieving. After three days, they departed.

Speaking of dogs and birds: if we get out early, before it's too hot for her, we can walk with Lucy to the creek. Of late, we're likely to see Turkey, a rafter of attractive hens. Yesterday I counted twelve. Approaching the water, we may scare up the Great Blue Heron, that grand, flapping dinosaur of a bird, maybe Canadian Geese or a Mallard. On a good morning—and come winter we can go all the time—we'll chart the Belted Kingfisher, creature of water, earth, and sky, swooping back and forth low over the mirroring surface. The thick body, dagger-like bill, rattling call directing our attention.

I've written before of the parliaments of young Screech Owl that, for many years, I summoned nightly from the woods with my mangled song, but never of the Great Horned Owl I once saw in the twilight, the tip of a cedar perpendicular under its weight. Where has the Meadowlark gone? We mustn't disregard the Bluebird on the wire, the Sharp-Shinned Hawk and wide-breasted and implacable Redtail, the small and colorful Kestrel with its own merciless dignity. Once only, the Oriole, but the Red-Winged Blackbird always to be found displaying its gaudy epaulets among the cattails. The Killdeer of the field dragging her wing as she leads me astray from her nest. The wake of Vulture—what strange and grotesque beauty those bald heads—at their meal or circling slowly overhead in announcement of the dead.

I embrace with reverence the geekiness of it all, adore the arcane and incantatory language: bevy of Bobwhite, murder of Crow, rafter, wake, parliament. Delicious. I could bore you all day with these wondrous intersections, this flitting wildness, the joy or pain over which I have no control as wings fill the air.

In All of Human History

. . . how rare it must be for a man to sit alone with his aging dog, listening together to the sounds of night, the covenant of solitary days ahead. Provisions of choice, his comfortable home, coin for his passage. Hours shaped only by whim, by imagination or the welcome lack of it. No village to support, no job, no woman, no war, no trial, no necessity for explanation or defense. No striving. Instead, the gradual and easy submission. To hold council only with his thoughts, be responsible only to the animal's need. There will be other days and nights for myth building, the naming of names, the fortification of his story, the errors of love. For now, in all of human history, the luxury of this moment, the privilege of an aimless tomorrow. He could sit here forever on this stoop in the cool reprieve, breathing the darkness with his panting friend, descendant of wolf.

Or, if not forever, a while longer.

Aubade with Wildlife and a Promise of Autumn

Enough nocturnes for now, we've surplus of dark reverie. When I look out into the possibilities of 6:30 a.m., two slim does stand golden in the light. A good beginning. They sense me, consider, trot for the woods.

Lucy smells her way into a different world, but the sun on the road is low and brilliant for us both. The chill air thrills. In only shorts and T-shirt, I am almost cold. September has been relentless, a cruel second August. No rain for weeks. Soon, the day will again punish, but now I shiver happily. We enter the shadows of the cedar grove, emerge behind three hen turkeys nearing the cleared creekside. The lead bird is enormous. While, sadly, I cannot report the song of the lark announcing the dawn, I can offer these ladies, and several others one by one flushed to the rock ledge opposite, plashing and flapping.

I can offer, too, the great blue heron that rises in my direction, its slow, deliberate propulsions above water stagnant with algae. It passes close, and I watch all the way. I can offer an implacable buzzard, high above, and another flustered turkey, spooked from a branch on the far bank into frantic, uncertain flight. A second hen follows, careering, wings beating. Who is not delighted by the ludicrous flight of turkeys? They themselves seem hardly to believe its plausibility. Among the fallen leaves, I select one long, perfect feather after another—brown, striped, each unique. A bouquet.

What silly creatures we are, how easy and fickle in our happiness. Good sleep, the risen sun, coolness on our skin, and hope is restored. Lucy and I see no humans. No penitent groggy from the night. No scrubbed believer steering toward worship. Did I mention it is Sunday? How pleasant, just us and the untamed. When we return up the drive, a new doe stands taut in the yard, head turned, watching us with her dark eyes, glowing in a circle of sunlight between the trees. When she begins to move away, I see her limp, then her missing rear hoof, and I call out to our old friend Three Leg, named with affection. My god, I've not seen her since, what, spring? Perseverance, acceptance, joy. A wonderful deer, still alive.

Finally, what is an aubade without romance? While I cannot offer the passionate blush of youth, I nevertheless arrange my collected plumage in a simple vase. A gift for my beloved, who tomorrow returns.

Fawn

This first day of autumn, three times at least she has crossed the yard alone, three times the gangly lope for cover in one direction or the other when she spies me first. Those spindly legs, that laughably large fluff of bobbing tail—a little beauty.

Alone, as I mentioned. I shout words of welcome and comfort each time toward the turned ears as she hastens from me and each time, wisely, doesn't believe a word. I am still a rough man, capable and willing of violence against any who would harm her. But how can she know this? Danger is the lesson of the world. She bounds away the third time as the woods darken. I am, of course, helpless to help her.

Think of her in the night, her blanket of grass, the small heart rapid. This waning harvest moon, still a lucent blade, lengthening the shadows. Where is her mother? Her brothers and sisters? How may this end but in the inevitable manner?

Lust

After Sienna explains, since they can't understand the pressure families put on girls, that *guys* will never understand her short story, and Kalie corrects the professor that having an affair and the *thought* of having an affair are indeed morally equivalent (I'd suggested the latter was known as "imagination"), I counter with the non sequitur that even Jimmy Carter, in his famous *Playboy* interview, admitted to having "lust in his heart," a defense which elicits the stony response, highlighted by a single ambiguous guffaw, it rightly deserves.

With that, another day's learning complete, the hour releases us to our mini "Fall Break" (which I scorned when implemented but now fully endorse). We distribute next week's stories—*clockwise to the left, please*—as I wish them all well, remind them to beware the police, and in no time am outside the building, touching the blue horseshoe for luck, swinging my briefcase like a shield, and taking the shortest angle through the walnut grove (no pregame festivities this week). A single robin on a branch, then a pair! A mockingbird! An acquisitive squirrel! The heat wave has relented, they forecast, until Sunday, and I'm in the T-bird, firing the indefensibly huge engine, top rising and folding at the tilt of a switch, and thinking ahead to a pink sky of twilight, earlier every day, a waxing three-quarter moon, the rollicking dog set free. And, ah, the myriad possibilities of dinner carry-out: spicy pho with flank steak and tripe? Moo shu pork with rich hoisin sauce? Or something less exotic—a hot roasted chicken to tear apart and really get our claws on?

Book Festival Aftermath

I had earmarked today as a free writing day during a hectic month and had in mind to recall the Great Tornado of 1974 that leveled Louisville on my ninth birthday. However, I gave a poetry reading at the big regional book festival yesterday and somehow neglected to anticipate its typical effect on me. Organized and thoughtful hosts (one-hundred-milliliter bottle of Jack Daniels in the swag bag), generous crowd, lovely October afternoon on the downtown plaza. I did a fair approximation of charm, got the laugh, and honestly—if obliquely—answered the requisite question on process. Even sold a few books, enough to pay for parking.

And found the entire event, as I always do, incredibly demoralizing, enervating, and just a little shameful. I look around, and everyone appears to be having a grand time, confident and congratulatory, easy among the tribe. Of course, to make matters worse I am here by choice. I *asked* to be invited and have no cause for complaint, no claim for grievance.

By the time I escape the city, the traffic, the descending weekend jollity, and am back home on my postage stamp of remaining woods, the best share of a beautiful autumn day, a day that will not return, has been butchered, wasted, lost. I get drunk as a necessity, medicine for the self-inflicted illness of public performance, medicine for the butcher. Lucy's eleventh birthday was two days ago, so that warrants another designer biscuit for her. When the full moon appears, low above the tree line, fat and custardy yellow, the world is not so small. I stand beneath, breathing in the silence, sipping my poison.

Honey Locust

The two rough-barked trunks, twenty-two and twenty-seven inches in diameter measured by my encircling hands, angle dramatically apart, a distancing begun, I assume, by mutual agreement, each sapling's grasp toward its fought portion of nourishing light. Now that I have cleared the perimeter of the property for a clean fence line, their crooked "V," thorny horns twisted into the open sky, is hard to miss. The honey locust is also commonly known, of course, as the thorny locust, and now that the feather-like, pinnate leaves have yellowed and fallen, the thorns clumped in unruly threat up the bare trunks are impressive. I have collected individual thorns eight inches in length. Once hardened and red, one may pass through the sole of a shoe with ease. That, of course, is a benign example of the violence possible.

The honey locust gets its name, I have read, from the sweet taste of the pulp within its large seed pods. A pulp used as traditional medicine but also, I further read, capable of a palatable tea when properly extracted and brewed. The original purpose of the thorns? Perhaps to ward off giant sloths, short-faced bears, and musk oxen, megafauna of the Pleistocene, though they do little to deter today's more meticulous deer. Due to its quick, aggressive growth and tolerance of urban degradations of soil, the honey locust—relatively short-lived at only a century or so—is considered a "weed" tree while also being a popular ornamental. That most of these latter varieties are cultivated without thorns epitomizes the banality of the human species.

No thorns? No thornbird, a final and magnificent song rising from its impaled breast. No thorns? No mocking crown for the martyr-king.

As I noted, in the newly tidied landscape, against a canvas of cedar fence, the ugly "V" of my two locusts is unmistakable and, if you're paying attention, hard to miss. Yes, I said mine, with affection. On a good day, I repeatedly claim their dangerous, craggy beauty. On a good day, I pay attention.

Trespass

The autumn light fails fast as I step over the rusted fence row, maneuver quickly between mounds of bulldozed earth and pyres of discarded lumber, onto the back-porch scaffolding and out of view of the street. By the end of the next work day, the masonry will be complete, in the days after that doors hung and latched. In the meantime, the words exposed on plywood, in a crude hand, might as well be scrawled in blood. To the left of the door: *The perverse of heart shall be far from me. I will have nothing to do with what is evil. Psalms 101:4.* And to the right, soon buried beneath jagged rows of mortar and brick: *No one who practices deceit shall dwell in my house. No one who utters lies shall continue before my eyes. Psalms 101:7.*

God almighty. For whom are these warnings intended, these incantations, these curses to be hidden forever? I cross into the murky interior, the skeleton of framing. Below my feet, drawn in the same unstable hand on the threshold of raw subfloor, by the prophet on his knees: *In your patience possess ye your souls. Luke 21:19.* I am inside, hidden in my transgression, breathing in night's arrival, smelling the cut of the saw. Invitations of the tomb. The Eve of the Dead is only days away, but already I am ghost, I am other, unsubstantiated, and move silently between the small hollow rooms. This, amidst the clearing we fought against and lost. This, the construction we opposed. Soon to be inhabited. At eye level, proclaimed along its crooked path, dimly legible and fading: *Whoso privily slandereth his neighbor, him I will cut off. Him that hath a high look and proud heart I will not suffer.*

Recipe: *Cajeta*/Goat's Milk Caramel

Unpasteurized quart from Goat Milk Lady down the road at Dogwood Creek Farm, that's the local flavor. Teaspoon of baking soda to lower the browning temperature of the milk, congenial science. Cup of sugar. For French influence, often invited, always welcome, fat black vanilla bean brought back in bundle from Provence, split and scraped. Healthy pinch of coarse Camargue salt. That is all that is required for alchemy.

Well, also the ingredient of a free morning, freely surrendered, the beginning of a long weekend with no commitments beyond those one chooses. October weather's come a month late, but it's come, and the old dog is frisky. Of course, patience is required. The meditative stirring, charmingly undemanding of anything save attention. The sweet milk frothing as it begins to color, the softening halves of pod, the aromatic specks of remnant seed. This will be an hour of your life, its currency spent as well in this manner as most, better than many. The agency of the task, the transformation to a commodity of pleasure, a gift to be given.

The back feels good, the body amenable. Stand your ground and stare into the cauldron: the thickening, the darkening, the swirling pattern of steady motion. And, at last, the glowing volcanic golds, four cups reduced to one, the magic. The effervescing enterprise, the last anxious moments until instinct tells you. Oh, the rich reward, voluptuous heat too hot for the tongue, morning opening to afternoon, to all the world has left, whatever sweetness, whatever time. Forget everything you've tasted before.

Note to My Wife, Her Morning Spent
at the Writers Conference

I spent mine, as I announced last night that I would, at the realty auction, farm parceled into three lots, owners moved on to the next thing. Not my entire morning, it turned out, as barely thirty minutes are required to change a life, or thirty chilly minutes not to, to edge over the cliff or just rubberneck. We stood loosely grouped around the revival tent, the podium, the barker with his microphone and repetitive chant, his interspersed scripture of opportunity slipping away. I doubt you know that auctioneering is also known as bid calling, auction cry, and, most endearingly, cattle rattle.

Bidding numbers clenched in hand, crafty with our tactics and limits, we waited for the gavel to end it. The house lot at 19.8 acres, did I mention, when I broached the subject and you refused? Did I mention no privacy fences, no redneck bonfires scaring us in the night? No ugly, intruding human voices? I wanted to argue the case of an implausible near-perfection for the three of us. A single story for the mutt's senior years, hardwood floors ready for rugs from that little shop we discovered in Savannah, the open kitchen for you, stone fireplace for me. Windows everywhere, and light. Handsome brown brick, poured porch and patio. No wood to indenture me as it has all these years. No wood to climb. No nails.

If allowed, I would have further extolled the gazebo with trellis of wisteria, the two whimsical rows of grapevine to prune and nurture as our own. The horrid wine to be made to torture friends in muscadine sacrament. Even the huge outbuildings crazily out of context of our history, one to be adapted to the painting/sculpture space I've always longed for. The other, to be anything. Those cedar woods to explore as the mutt enforced her new perimeter.

Why go on? It's just conjecture, indulgence, a hobby of self-punishment with extra to go around. The parcels sold. The house went first. I didn't look at the buyers. I didn't want to see them, anxious, whispering, living already that new life, with ten percent down today, balance due at closing. The price less than I'd imagined.

April 3, 1974

On April 3, 1974, Kentucky was struck by an incredible number of tornadoes—20—one more than had been sighted during the entire worst year on record. The grim toll of 71 deaths and 693 injured reflects the intense level of storm activity.

—*The Courier-Journal*

Standing by the plate glass windows inside Kroger, on Eastern Parkway, as shopping carts flew and spun in the air and assaulted cars, was perhaps not the most prudent place to congregate, but there we were, children and adults, gawking at the minor carnage, entranced by the beast of the suddenly dark sky.

Our last stop, to pick up something needed for the evening's festivities. A stressful afternoon of fun nearly over. Mom had picked me up early from school—a half day's hooky, with permission!—to take me out for a birthday lunch. Probably, we went to Kingfish for the free fish sandwich offered on the occasion. I recall us driving along the interstate, the increasingly dire and immediate forecasts on the radio. In my imagination, the light is eerily bright, the grass glowing, the sky silent and calm. If we saw a funnel, we were to pull to the shoulder and flatten ourselves on the ground wherever possible. We lived in Audubon Park, a neighborhood a few miles from downtown Louisville, a self-proclaimed bird sanctuary named after the painter, on Linnet Road. In three weeks, we'd hold our annual Dogwood Festival, pride of the community. The flowering limbs lit at night, the women costumed in antebellum dresses waving from front porches. Audubon Park was known for, and proud of, its abundance of mature trees. Today, that pride seemed a curse. What was happening? What already had?

The carts landed and the worst seemed to have passed. We headed for the Buick and the short drive home. I don't recall if we were silent in the car, if the radio still blared its warnings, if Mom tried to console me or herself. As we entered the park, curving slowly up Cardinal Drive beneath a clear sky, grid of streets passing—Cross Bill, Dove—as we approached our own, the sight was bleak, the road a riot of branches. Chickadee. Shattered windows. Century-old trunks split like kindling. Oriole. A crushed roof, its open scar of joists. A collapsed chimney of stone. Thrush. There would be no Dogwood Festival this year, maybe ever again. I don't recall either of us crying, but maybe we were in shock. Linnet. Our street impassable. We parked in the lot of the country club—of which we were never members—and began the two-block climb between torn roots and canted trees toward the house, my parents' dream, where they had finally settled to raise their boys. Climbed toward whatever remained.

Despite the wreckage, our house was virtually untouched. A mangled gutter. A missing fascia board. My father and two older brothers were home. I remember the days and weeks that followed, the saws, the digging out, the subdued conversations between neighbors, but little of our safe reunion that afternoon. Mostly I recall that, without electricity, the ice cream melted and we had none for my cake. At nine, I was bitter about that. I made a wish anyway, as if one were still required.

Double Jeopardy

We married on my wife's birthday, so this day in October arrives circled on the calendar, a lodestone, a scrutiny. I sometimes wonder if doubling down was a good idea. For me, the pressure is on, the fat's in the fire. Duck fat, typically. We'll start with flutes of prosecco, a general toast to good fortune, better yet to smoked trout eggs with crème fraîche on buckwheat blinis. Move on to seared foie gras and diced apple on a mix of spring greens with a dribble of apple cider reduction I made yesterday. For the main plate, a moulard duck breast with a toasted fennel seed and chile dry rub that I like for ribeyes and believe will work. I have faith. The ideology: fat rendered, skin crisped in my infallible Lodge skillet, windows open for the smoke. Breast rested and, knock on wood, sliced medium rare and fanned over pasta bowls of asparagus risotto, the latter a nod to last summer's holiday in the Piemonte. So, I guess an Italian red just makes sense. I'll take a look at what's on hand. For dessert a disgustingly rich chocolate cake—with my wife's imprimatur—fashioned after our wedding confection, a side of homemade goat-milk ice cream lovingly made for my lactose-intolerant love. Maybe skip the digestif for a cup of good decaf (if you quote me on the latter, I'll deny both the oxymoron *and* the decaf).

In other words, keeping it light and simple. There's more to a shared life than food and drink, after all, and privilege grows tiresome, excess exhausting. Prior to culinary battle, I sit quietly, perhaps even reflectively, in my study, both windows ajar, listening to a faint but steady patter of rain after weeks of drought. I hear, too, the dog gnawing her new bone in the living room, my wife squeaking in the bathtub. All sounds I like. Yes, wrapped gifts decorate the table, a vase of yellow tulips. A card, as yet unopened, promising pleasantness for the duration. So far, a passable performance. If the mood arises, and I feel equal to the challenge (i.e., two martinis in), a recitation of Neruda may even be in the wings. We'll see how the evening plays.

The dog arrives with her bone, growls a warning, and drops, back to the work of stripping it clean. I am reminded that tomorrow—as I am well aware—brings another day. But not yet.

The Poets' Global Advocacy Group
against Noise and Light Pollution

We argue only for the simplest—the profoundest—of rights:

Our Silence.

Our Darkness.

Grasshopper

I am back home at last, grateful for my habitual walk east along Highway 96 to shake off the days and miles. 96 is busier, more "developed," less picturesque every year, but it's convenient from my street, familiar, and still relatively rural. Lightning, the old swaybacked horse I fed carrots (he preferred them to sugar cubes) for ages, to the suspicion of his double-wide owners, is long gone, abandoned washer/dryer and mattress in his stead. I was told, by someone claiming to know horses, Lightning snapped at me because he knew I had food for him in my pockets. Well, I could be a bit temperamental myself. We got along well enough.

For company I pass a large grasshopper unmoving on the shoulder on the road, facing the two lanes as if with intent. It's a peculiar position, and when I turn at the gravel drive that denotes the one-mile turnaround, I wonder if the insect's dead. Passing again, I stop to investigate. A handsome specimen. Vivid, luminous green. Muscular hind legs miniature catapults in repose. It looks healthy enough, so I inquire about its odd location and, with little forethought, nudge with a shoe. It flurries into the air, twirls and loops, landing in the middle of the far lane of the country road. Instinctively, I look right. Of course cars are coming. Shit. I tense and wait.

One. Two. A third. Each passes over the damned thing without crushing it, although the body's buffeted around. Assault over, I jog across to apologize and enact rescue, but the grasshopper is on its side, ripped apart, oozing, legs and antennae slack. The tornado of the automobiles.

I was home, another death on my hands. For what? For stupid play? For insolence? An adult grasshopper may live two months. A foolish man, many decades. It was a fine, warm October afternoon. I stood there, staring and culpable, the gooey corpse at my feet, until the next speeding shape appeared in the distance.

Uninvited

The only thing that excites Lucy more than Claudia asking whether she'd like to walk to the "beach" (i.e., the cleared strip, pebbly-soiled and abundant with mussel shell, alongside the creek), is if I also tag along. Family affair. When the weather's cold enough and the timing's right—i.e., we're likely to make it the whole way—I am usually invited. For us humans, the trek's excitement in ascending order is thus: turkey, deer, mallard/Canadian goose (tie), blue heron, kingfisher, and the coveted prize, rarest of all, otter. Lucy's priority remains more focused: the occasional glimpse of our neighbor "Aunt" Emily, who lives adjacent to the water. If we three are together on a morning or afternoon jaunt and Emily approaches from her house as lagniappe, Lucy's joy is unbridled. This is as good as life gets without food.

So, I was mildly surprised when I heard the proffered invitation, subsequent jangling of leash and bell, zip of coat, and storm door opening, all without my name being called. I was sitting right where I am at this moment, perhaps sit too much but often anxious for interruption, especially any involving trips to the beach.

You never know. In recent years, Lucy is inscrutable but decisive about how far she's willing to go before she won't budge, so maybe the expedition is exploratory, just a walk to Emily's mailbox, and my exclusion not a snub. I'm distracted enough to pour more coffee and go meet them upon return down the lane. First, I sweep the porch free of leaves. I sip my coffee. Take my time before tackling our long gravel drive in my slippers, shorts, and sweatshirt. It's colder than I expect. When I clear the trees, I immediately see in the distance Claudia in her puffy brown coat and hood, and leading the way the tiny but unmistakable white shape of my girl nosing along, smelling her way through the green world. They vanish and reappear among the stand of cedars, inching along toward their goal. It's far too late to catch up, even if I were dressed for it, even if I were invited, to those two little shapes that make up so much of my lucky life. Sure, an explanation will be required. I take another warming sip and turn for the house. They'll be back.

November

From the woods, a clarion striking as of hammer hard onto nail, and such force can only announce, I am certain, the enormous pileated woodpecker I saw from the kitchen window last week. In twenty years, perhaps a half dozen sightings here on the property of that reclusive bird. I rise from the porch swing to investigate. Some welcome cold days have finally arrived, even some rain. I navigate fallen leaves with what clumsy stealth I can muster and approach the tree line. A shape rises, swoops, and lands on a nearby hackberry. The spotted breast and black crescent, flash of red on the nape are unmistakable: nope, only a flicker. I rousted it from our decrepit old catalpa, my favorite tree in the yard. An assault on a dead branch of trunk explains the percussion, and the flicker is itself a muscular bird.

This morning, to the east of the house, I saw the young buck again. Lucy's barking brought me to the door. His mate nibbled privet at the edge of the drive, the doe's coat already turned winter silver. The buck nearby in the shadows, a flash of shoulder, of small but fine antlers. They are a handsome couple, and I welcome them and wish for their safety.

These recent days, I have not felt well in body or mind. A few routine dark thoughts better unspoken, but really no excuse. Just a gray pall settled in, a tired discouragement. Best to keep to myself and my mouth shut. Lucy, however, tends to intuit and absorb my moods, good or bad, which further concerns me. The flicker is a help, as are the cautious deer, as is the catalpa stubborn for life, and the white slant of autumn light.

Hawk

The November morning unseasonably cold, around 20°F, and I relished its punishment on my exposed hands and neck. A poor parking spot on the edge of campus had left me with a hike. I was late for the early class in what would be an arduous day. As I walked, distracted in thought, along the border of the president's mansion, I heard the feathered shuffling, the leaf-rattling hop from one branch to another, peripherally sensed the movement of shadowed contour. A quick descent over frozen ground, careful through a dusting of snow, and I could see clearly the enormous redtail, its broad, tawny shoulders turned to me, unmoving on the thick limb of a squat old chestnut. I moved closer, certainly violating the range of space between us. The hawk should have spread its wings and risen but did not. I moved closer, incautiously close until I stood only feet from the low branch. Chestnuts, glossy and dangerous in their spiky casings, littered the lawn. The redtail turned its head—the black hook of beak, the glowing implacable eye focused on me—otherwise still did not move. I thought of Jeffers, of course, but detected no "unable miserable," only that deliberate, restive power. I saw no prey in its talons, could think of no other reason why it remained. The tree was beautiful, the hawk, beautiful. No need for metaphor or augury. I joined in its stillness, exhaling clouds of breath. If I'd had time, I no doubt would have trespassed longer, moved even more foolishly toward possible retribution. But, as I mentioned, I was late for class, late to deliver my thoughts on a protagonist whose dreams and ideals had betrayed him.

In the afternoon, obligations complete, light already fading, air colder still, I hurried back to the tree, to the bare limb.

"Beware of perfect moments . . ."

. . . Spalding Gray cautioned me on a sunny November afternoon a decade before he jumped into the East River and committed suicide. We were in a froufrou hotel on West End Avenue in Nashville, Spald lying on the bed, hands across his chest, staring at the ceiling, talking, talking, talking. I sat in a chair bedside. The faux therapy setting was unnerving, and I finally coaxed him downstairs to the bar.

I'm uncertain why, two weeks ago, the phrase came back to me on a clear night twenty-five years later. November had inexhaustibly arrived. I was reclined on the lawn, legs crossed, leaning back on my hands in the dry leaves. Lucy beside me alert to smells and shadows. Gorgeous moon, two days from full, clearing the cedars. An idyllic scene, though one unmarred by any conceit of perfection. My well-worn flaws and distractions offering, again, their sure protection.

Still, a pleasant moment shared with my happy old dog, with earth and heaven. And now it is Thanksgiving, a day the three of us—man, woman, canine—have come to enjoy spending alone. A crisp morning, sunny. All the prep work complete, well enough save one butcher knife wounding. What feast without blood? Soon I will truss the bird, begin the mesmerizing spin of the rotisserie. When the turkey has lightly browned, I will brush the beast, as it turns, with my standby of truffle butter and maple syrup, caramelize the skin to bronze.

At an early hour—the "holiday exception"—I will open the bottle of Laphroaig my wife recently gave me, release that fist of peaty smoke and pour a generous splash over ice. From the front-porch swing, watch the early sunset. Lucy nearby and attentive to her own concerns. A toast to Spalding, if I remember to, would do no harm. No good, either.

Open Casket

Yes, I could offer my opinions on such a ritual, describe the state of the body, or the widow dressed dashingly in black blouse with flared sleeves and gold lamé cuffs. How, as we waited in line for our turn at condolence, one old friend after another approached with smiles and hugs. It was a big crowd, big success, folks we'd not seen in ages. Yes, everyone had aged twenty years overnight, but the consensus, assuming one's health, was that retirement was the way to go, a grand life well-earned.

I could tell you Bill was a good man, and mean it, that we'd shared adjacent offices, talked a lot of sports. I could report that even in his sixties he was fit, an avid tennis player, or recall years later our encounter in a grocery parking lot, his sallow skin, the unnatural bloating of the face. Truth told, if I'd seen him after that, I would have avoided him.

I'd known many people in that room for decades, the affairs, betrayals, rises and falls and rebirths, rumored or witnessed. Maybe even some dusty dirt on me. Who cared, now? The details felt not only tacky, but unnecessary. Suffice to say the tone was festive. Jokes were told. Dates tallied. All agreed how great we all looked. My collar choked me. The holiday season was in swing and this was a reunion of family. Further from the casket, the jollity increased. In the hallway, the son telling tales, it was practically a party going on.

Outside, I freed my collar, loosened the noose of necktie. As we drove, already the darkness coming in. Incredibly, less than an hour had passed. We had no food in the house but didn't care, didn't stop. That's enough. Just know we wanted to get home. Our headlights lit the doe, legs shattered, that had lain crumpled in the rain since yesterday. Then we were over the bridge and almost there.

III: WINTER

bling; Musso & Frank; Quebec City; Rudolph revealed; disquisitions on gin; unnamed foreboding; murmuration; marrow bones; suicide memory; Stan the Man

Gloriously Alone

Three December days, calm and cool and bright. A gorgeous forecast. The proverbial cupboard groaning under rich food and drink. Three days of roughhousing with dog, sitting with white winter sunlight on face and hands. The windchime easy, melodious. Chickadees busy at the feeder. No holiday commerce, no workplace degradation, no council but canine. Answering the telephone on a case-by-case basis. The enchanting absence of human voice. A good novel—mystery as yet unresolved—on the end table. Then, too, the needed repairs I've no intention of beginning, the final essays unread in their file. All this open time to breathe in. This giddiness. After everything, can it be so simple?

Bling

I've just returned to its velvet box a 1902 Morgan silver dollar, obverse a profile of Liberty, reverse an eagle with spread wings. It's a handsome coin, heavy, in nice condition, and happens, I am told, to have been in my father's father's pocket on the day he died of a stroke several years before I was born, hardly older than I am now. 1902 was his birthdate. My parents gave me the coin as an unexplained gift not too long ago, but not before encircling it in a bevel and attaching a silver chain. Although I eschew jewelry, including a wedding band, my mother seemed to genuinely believe I would wear the necklace—perhaps with a silk shirt, open down the front?—was surprised and vaguely hurt when I suggested not.

They are dispensing the wealth, distributing the legacy as time draws nigh. My last visit to Kentucky, I had just arrived. We were sitting in their modest sunroom with drinks and snacks, when my dad said he wanted to "talk serious for a second." Uh-oh. Cut to the chase: Would I like his diamond ring? A gold ring with a prominent cluster of stones that my mother saved up for and gave him thirty years ago. He'd hesitated to mention this because, with all the crazy travel I do, someone would probably take it from me, such an imaginative and astounding idea that it requires no discussion. (Okay, just a little: the assumption, again, that I would wear it. Not just on nominal "special occasions," but all the time—the shadowed alleyways of Vietnam, the crowded medinas of Morocco, the candy aisle of Walgreens. And finally, that I am a naïve chump with an x on his chest.) Despite feeling touched and unnerved by this offer/challenge, and just a bit amused by its solemnity, I had no idea how to reply. (I liked, though, the stealth. No booty for my older brothers.) Well, the relic was produced. After Dad's arthritis, they'd resized for Mom, but the ring proved too weighty. It fit my little finger. I twirled the gold and sparkling gems below the knuckle and considered my new gangsta look with a sip of martini. Getting through airport security would be a bear, but on the other side I'm sporting my pinky ring and Liberty necklace, showin' the bling in Hanoi, in Marrakesh! Poet in the house, bitch!

I returned the ring to my father's dresser when I left. When the day comes, I'll be pleased to have it. As I will the coin, once my wife's jeweler removes the bevel. For my lack of flash and style, my mother's bewilderment, I can only apologize.

Musso & Frank

With only one scheduled reading in LA, I had time for roaming and possibly a bit of mischief. Regarding the former, I'd checked off Griffith Park, okay, and the tar pits, done. But this morning I was truly geeking out. I'd unexpectedly passed De Longpre Avenue in East Hollywood, did a quick maneuver with the rental, and drove rubbernecking up and down the block, trying to recall the number of Bukowski's bungalow. The houses looked nicer, tidier than I'd expected. Even so.

Then on to the main event of brunch at Musso & Frank with my friends Ron and Bianca. Here were the crimson banquettes. Here—delivered on a tray by a resigned and careful old man in signature white shirt, black bowtie, and red jacket—my morning martini with its famous sidecar. The waiter shuffled away, his stooped shoulders all he intended to tell me of a world that had brought us to this.

At that moment if Faulkner or Bob Mitchum had ambled to the gleaming bar for the day's first drop, or Bacall had sashayed toward the Back Room without one head bothering to turn, I could hardly have been happier. What great, kitschy fun. Something else, too. Regret, or a loneliness I couldn't precisely name. Something irretrievable.

Even so, my martini was superb.

Manoir Sur-le-Cap

Sipping a smooth but woodsy Québécois gin, a plate of smoked salmon and sturgeon and a good mystery on the side table, warm in soft flannel I sit still in the rocking chair before the fire. Downstairs—it's a three-story suite, four if you count the mud room for boots and coats—my wife soaks in the whirlpool tub. An afternoon of walking in the cold and snow of the Plains of Abraham, of shopping for gifts, of hot mulled wine balanced in stiff hands at the German Christmas Market. In an hour, a reservation at a favorite, intimate restaurant, a taxi to guide us there, coin for every cost and generous tips. What more to say, really, regarding this life of absurd privilege? I am practiced in excess, good at sensual pleasure, but also at the dark mood, the rent moment, the blade artfully delivered. I taste the botanicals on my tongue, watch the fire writhe and gasp.

Then, as is my habit these past five years of holiday, I walk to the double doors of the balcony, open them toward me, and step into the pleasant sting of early night. I gaze past the blue-lit spruce perennially on display, over a white rooftop and across the St. Lawrence, a river I fear and love. On the opposite shore, atop the hill, the scattered lights of Lévis, better from a distance. The ferries keep the river from freezing, break passage through shelves of ice. A boat crosses now, slow, deliberate, its reflection small on the black water. The river's majestic indifference and beatitude of danger.

Christmas Piece

The armadillo immigrated to Tennessee only a handful of years ago, its mission to die on our highways, and this one I drag by the tail from roadside to brown grass, leave a crimson silhouette. That's nothing to the morning shock of filling the bird feeder from the plastic garbage container in the shed. Yes, I'd seen the gnawed hole in the duct tape, but after a lifetime of fighting the Rodent Wars gave it little credence until something heavy fell from the funnel of sunflower shells. My first startled instinct—unfortunately, I'm serious—that it was a severed squirrel's head, that I'd been "sent a message," *Godfather*-style. Rather, a field mouse soft and cute as advertised, though no longer part of any seasonal rhyme. Other than squinched-up eyes and tiny raised claws, peaceful, disinterred from its grave of seed.

Perhaps that's enough death for the day. Virgin births are hard to come by. The Quebec City of three days ago—10°F the daily high, drifting snowflakes, icicles in my mustache, carolers in hats and long coats of fur—is a world away. Here in paradise it's a balmy and unnerving 70°F, and wearing only shorts and light jacket I return from my walk in a sweat. At the creek, a great blue heron rises. One, two, three, four turtles dive from a bare log. Turtles, in December! Distantly, I hear but do not see the rattle of the belted kingfisher, creature of earth, sky, and water, of luck and fortune. Perhaps these intersections, together with a raised dram from a hidden half bottle of Laphroaig, bolstered by Claudia's offering of roast duck, will serve as ballast to a holy day in unholy times. And a bone for Lucy, of course.

Reindeer Games:
Rudolph as Homoerotic Fantasia

Nativity

Donner, packing an enormous rack (of antlers), staring down in confusion and anger at his newborn, the infant's blinking cherry of a nose. Will the boy grow out of it? Santa—squire in deer-stalker and herringbone jacket—arriving in a surprise visit, delivering the scarcely concealed threat: "Let's hope so." The father's further denial: "You'll be a normal little buck like everybody else . . ." Smearing the kid's bulb with mud. Even Sam the Snowman, narrator, concurring that "for the first year, the Donners did a pretty good job of hiding Rudolph's, uh, uh, *nonconformity* . . ."

Little Helpers

The elves, rarely seen outside of Santa's castle, jolly and indistinguishable in its toy-making sweatshop. "Papa" Santa, oligarch and alpha human of Christmas Town, visibly uncomfortable and impatient during their seasonal song of praise to him.

(Def. *eunuch*: "A man castrated to perform a specific social function." Def. *castrato*: "A type of classical male singing voice equivalent to that of a soprano.")

Only lonely elf Hermey, soon to join Rudolph in his Misfit Trio, only Hermey, dentist manqué creepily "fixing" mouths of dolls during off-hours, shock of flamboyant blond hair intimating his effeminate vitality, only he demurring, at cost of ridicule and mockery.

Reindeer Games

The randy, spirited Fireball, Rudolph's self-appointed new pal, leading his naïf friend to the games that "make antlers grow," encouraging him to check out the does, first to recoil, face contorted, when Rudolph's grotesque costume proboscis inevitably pops off. "Get away! Get away from me!" The brutish old-school coach of the games, sleigh veteran Comet, quick to lead in Rudolph's humiliation and announce his banishment, egging on the yearlings in their jeers. "From now on, gang, we won't let Rudolph join in *any* reindeer games, right?"

As to the adorable and too-good-to-believe Clarice, unwavering in approbation for Rudolph's "handsome" real nose?

A beard from the beginning?

Exile

Rudolph and Hermey, paired by chance, recognizing each other immediately, celebrating in song being "different from the rest . . ." Spending their first night together in the arctic wasteland outside of Christmas Town, next morning the bearish Yukon Cornelius appearing on cue, rescuing the youngsters by pulling them by their exposed asses from a snowbank. Yukon Cornelius, master of the brutal terrain, Yukon of nimble tongue forever exploring the tip of his pickax for elusive gold, Yukon who has lived alone, forever resigned to disappointment: "Nuthin'." Yukon, expert on the Abominable Snow Monster, rescuing his new companions again, Rudolph and both orally compulsive soulmates escaping by the older man's skill and quick thinking. The three casting off adrift on a wedge of ice across a dark and inhospitable sea. "Yukon Cornelius scores again!" the protector announcing, going third-person.

The Abominable Snow Monster

A.k.a. a "Bumble," a hairy, raging libido, not too smart, kind of cute in a bestial way. Drawn to yet apparently enraged by Rudolph's nose. Ultimately rendered toothless by Hermey's wrenching pliers, the "dentist's" first patient tortured, emasculated. (To lure the Bumble from his lair, Hermey, on Yukon's advice, on his knees, oinking like a pig. "Oink. Oink.") "You're looking at one humble Bumble!" Yukon trumpeting joyfully, later dragging the monster by leash into Santa's castle. The Bumble's final ignominy as he is made to place a banal and gaudy star atop the Christmas tree, the same tree from which Yukon Cornelius's dream of precious metals hangs as cheap tinsel decoration. (Too much? Note juxtaposition of Sam the Snowman's earlier performance of "Silver and Gold.")

Speaking of Sam the Snowman

With his holly-adorned derby hat, tartan vest, and umbrella (rotund body otherwise naked and visibly lacking genitalia), a bit of a dandy? A misfit himself never allowed into Santa's circle? Asexual chronicler of truths, peering from outside through a frosty window at festivities that exclude him?

The Island of Misfit Toys

"My name is all wrong. No child wants to play with a 'Charlie in the Box.'"

(Among Wikipedia's list of LGBT slang terms for men: "Charlie.")

A cowboy riding an ostrich. A choo-choo with square wheels on its "caboose." A bird that swims. Loads of identity confusion and frustration on the island. Who created such toy misfits? Who responsible for their exile? The singing elves? Santa as notional savior? No one talking, but lamenting together in their own song that "on the island of unwanted toys, [they'll] miss all the fun with the girls and the boys."

Rudolph and company, washed upon that shore, denied sanctuary but granted shelter for the night. King Moonracer, Aslan the Lion wannabe, entreating for Santa's intervention "to find little boys and girls who would be happy" playing with his castaways, then setting up the ménage à trois in a cute-as-a-button dream cottage, pink. Pink curtains. Pink sheets on the small bed they share.

Earlier, the water pistol that "shoots jelly" exploding its mess into young Hermey's astonished face.

"Christmas Is Canceled."

Flash forward. The "storm of storms" arriving. Santa, fretting over weather and "that silly elf song driving [him] crazy," unable to eat. The broken Bumble hauled in obedient and enslaved. The sum of Santa's holiday ideology a megalomaniacal fever dream of distribution and hyper-consumerism. No toy delivery, no Christmas.

At last, the man seeing the light. Rudolph's nose incandescent, uncontrollable, squeaking wildly, virtually throbbing. Old man blinded into epiphany, hyperbole, delusion. "You and that wonderful nose of yours. Ho ho. From what I see now, that'll cut through the murkiest storm they can dish out." One shining, revealed nose against the blowing tumult of the "storm of storms" that is the world. The unnamed "they" a cry of paranoia.

In quick succession: Santa fat, bloated, spoon-fed by Mama, recognized: "Now, *that's* my Santa." Summoned, the eunuch-elves dressing Papa in traditional costume of lush red velvet gorgeously trimmed in white fur.

Yukon Cornelius landing his axe, licking heartily, tasting "peppermint. What I've been searching for all my life . . . wa-*hoo*!" The force of his excitement knocking Hermey backward onto the snow, the boy's pretty *o* of an amazed mouth widening suddenly into a lipstick smile red as candy cane. Abandoned by the assimilated Rudolph, the two now a couple?

Santa, after an impromptu landing, magically accommodating all of the misfit toys into his single bag. The entourage airborne again, eunuch-elf throwing one misfit after another from the sleigh into the raging night, each with only a small open umbrella for navigation/survival (shades of Sam the Snowman?). *Only* the misfit toys discarded to plummet into blackness. (Should've stayed on the island?)

During the massacre, Santa glassy-eyed, working himself into a lather, whipping the sleigh team, repeatedly barking a demented "Merry Christmas!" to no one in particular. Finally: "Rudolph: full power!"

Panning shot: Rudolph a glowing speck in the distance, leading the team on a seeming collision course with a gleaming and indifferent moon. Christmas saved.

> "It was the night *after* Christmas,
> and all through the house . . ."

This listless valley between final onslaughts of celebration. Numbed by cozy hearth, blurred with food and drink, punch-drunk from fraught family cheer. The lights and bells subdued, vanquished to an attic corner. Friends with the generosity, or ennui, not to call, not to write, not this week. A favor you return. Even retailors half-hearted in their closing offers, the charities' pleas desultory. Time without escape, calendar held hostage, dull hours, leaden skies. Brain sluggish, body unresponsive. The year ended with a thud.

Finally, one last strained hoorah, last teary sentiment, sloppy song, midnight with fireworks sputtering in cold rain, then thank god, passing out in bed—it's over. Just come to in the morning, obligation fulfilled to feel like hell, and it's over. Over! Can of black-eyed peas for luck, can of collard greens for wealth, a vague resolution a lot like last time's crumpled in your pocket. Striding into the maw of a new year likely to eat you alive, relieved to death to finally be here, go back to work. Season survived and safe again to turn on the radio.

Notes on the Closing Year

The rain that hammered the house through the night suited and accommodated my mood. I sat outside in the dark, listening to the assault, thinking deeply of nothing. This morning, the porch I scrubbed clean last week is a map of muddy paw prints, an abstract artwork scoffing human effort. White December sunlight, as if the storm had cleansed the system. I wouldn't say its clarity admonishes, but it doesn't enlighten, either, and my mood remains unchanged. Restive. Impatient. Something whispers to me. Whispers that it doesn't matter. A lucky year even by extravagant standards: health, wealth, travel, folks ailing but alive, Lucy showing her age only by an economy of movement of which I approve. I look down past my newly scarred left hand. What will the next year bring? My suspicions trouble me. Throw down the bones and heed their warning. For the moment, perhaps best to surrender to the sunlight and winter air, a country walk. The passing terrain, what's been lost or discarded roadside. Count the paces between mailboxes. Keep the head empty. Incredible, the things I find when not looking.

Ginspiration/Ginocide/DisinGinuous

I have a martini and I feel, once more, real.
—Anne Sexton

One martini is all right. Two are too many,
and three are not enough.
—James Thurber

In my cookbook *The Poet's Guide to Food, Drink, & Desire*, I elaborated on the culture of the martini, its ideology, the transformative power of its first kiss, and the principle "dos" and numerous unforgiveable "don'ts" of its correct preparation. Oh, and waxed lyrical on my personal history with the beast. *Vide supra* for details, thank you.

So a new year is upon us, tooth and claw, and I have been hitting the Bombay and Beefeaters pretty good throughout the stultifying holiday season. What is it about gray, drizzly days of a nascent January that bully one into stale self-reflection? The percussive music of the shaker, jitterbug of the wrist, torrent into frosted glass, glimmering arctic surface, stem raised delicately between fingertips toward parted lips . . . sigh. Has she begun to take more than she gives? A tedious line of thought. Churchill coughing cigar smoke of disappointment over one shoulder. Studs Terkel shaking his old head, fedora askew, over the other.

To begin last year, I suckered myself into a thirty-day challenge of total, gruesome sobriety. Top secret. Kept a journal that I swear on my grave no eyes but mine shall ever suffer. I had studied the augurs of the calendar, done the math: By beginning said folly on January 15, I wouldn't sacrifice too much of my vacation break. A few dull weeks, no social commitments, and the first classes of the semester for distraction. Bounding from purgatory on February 14, the tritest contrivance of romance reborn with joy.

I can laugh about it now. The days were slow. The slog toward and through happy hour, then afterward, over the hurdle, resignation settled in for the evening. I couldn't sleep, so after wife and dog retired to the back of the house I practiced an arcane drip method for brewing Vietnamese coffee, with a stir of sweetened condensed milk into a crystal goblet, and read Philip Roth voraciously, late into the winter night. A prolific author, Roth.

The distant day arrived: Happy Valentine's Day, sweetie! You've never looked more beautiful! Pour one up! Cheers!

I may do it again this year, just to suffer. An undefined, debilitating penance. I've a few more days to stare out at the rain, sip the sweet poison, consider the nuances. 2020, the Year of Our Lord of Clear Vision? We'll see.

Mr. & Mrs. Speck

I release a loud and leisurely yawn to the night and am taken back almost half a century. I believe my yawn to be a respectable effort, a fair representation of its type, but it pales beside the rolling, expansive, atonal crescendos of sound bellowed by Mr. Speck from his back porch, his gift to Audubon Park. Huge, ballooning calls, less lion than sea lion, offered throughout the day.

We moved to Linnet Road when I was five, next door to the Specks. I don't trust my memory of Mr. Speck's undershirts in summer, red flannels in winter, nor his bald head, nor his fleshy old-man odor, nor whether they never had visitors or perhaps a middle-aged daughter was involved. Hell, how old were the Specks, anyway, with their odd name and imposing brick house I can't recall stepping into in fourteen years? But I must have, mustn't I, into hallway or kitchen on the rare occasion? Mrs. Speck I see as a small, gray woman, perennially sour. And why wouldn't she be, with my basketball continually careening beyond the boundary of our drive and into her yard? How many broken lilies and tulips, abused stems of daffodils, garden seedlings crushed beneath the errant ball or the heel of its stealthy recovery? How miserable she must have been at my trampling of her fragile blooms and tender shoots. I tried to be careful. I'm certain I did. But in the heat of the game—even the game of one—the wild jump shot, the muscular rebound lost out of control . . . In all those years, no one ever thought to put up a modest fence just there at the edge of blacktop.

Or perhaps someone did. I'm foggy on that too. Now I have a recollection, real or invented, of jumping a decorative barrier and continuing right along in my reign of destruction as MVP of the All-Star All-Universe game. Who remains to say? The Specks are long dead, their spinster daughter as well if she existed, and how curious that I am the one to remember them, commit the two to lives however poor. They may have been a kind couple, loving, wounded, with a hard history. Or maybe not. The adult is encrypted to the child, something I think about more and more. But good lord, those yawns were impressive. I could hear them even from inside, in my bedroom on the far side of the house. Can hear them across nearly fifty years. Mr. Speck's tuneless song to the world. A lesson for the future, if I'd known how to listen.

Darkness

This winter condition, for lack of better phrase, remains on me. Perhaps not a darkness so much as a silence, a restive animal, an uninflected distance. I've no excuse, no right to it. Bright January afternoon. The world sunshine and roses. And yet. Walking the countryside makes no difference, the great texts, the austerity of the fast, the amateur's attempt at mindfulness. Certainly no discussion of a trite and popular rebirth. And not seasonal, either. The last time the fist seized me was on an island in Brazil. July. Heaven. Not a thing I would call depression, and certainly not despair, but a sort of . . . what? Wariness? An unspecified foreboding? Neither does it lack an ironic perspective, moments of humor and recognition. Whether the cause be chemical, mental, spiritual, or other is of no interest to me. I have learned to remain quiet—in breathing, in thought, in movement. To listen and wait. Trust the gestures. Better, too, all possible distance from the human comedy. As necessary: smile, nod, move away, reveal nothing. Keep the hands open and still. When it arrives at home, though, I feel bad for Lucy, so keenly attuned to my mood. I stroke her fur and ask patience. Assure her all will be well.

Murmuration

I'm only a few minutes from home, late to begin my trip, my mind elsewhere—the hours ahead, the failed night before—than on this familiar route past the county landfill, when the starlings appear in the sky. Several thousand birds, I would guess, in balletic formation, shifting crescents, ellipses, collective clouds of wing, twisting and urgent in their gracefulness, orchestrated, fluid, wild. The largest flocking I've ever witnessed—bravo!—rising above the denuded mountain of the dump, grotesque and alien landscape with ballpark and picnic grounds at its base. Driving by, it is lately advisable even in winter to keep one's windows raised. In August, the stench will choke you, cling to your clothes if you're fool enough to have the top down. No place to celebrate the wind in your hair, and every year the foulness expanding, sometimes now downwind for miles. I pull into the pitted lot of the Grab 'n' Go to watch the birds complete their formations. The shapes dissolve, disperse into the bare January treetops. I risk cracking my window, hold my breath, and listen to the discordant, gossipy racket in the distance. The starling, invasive bully, typically elicits little sympathy or affection, much less awe. What faith remains as it was? I turn the car around, wait my turn as the disgorged garbage trucks rumble out into the world for another load, then merge back onto Highway 266, west and north.

Quite Possibly, the Best Moment of the Day

Ah, to remain in bed beneath the winter comforter, listening to a companionable rain tattooing the deck and dripping from the leaky gutter I've neglected. Beside me, the old dog stretched and content, agreeable to my lounging. The house empty and silent. A so-called work day, all those of merit long since into the fray of their achievements. I close my eyes. Live each full, deliberate inhalation of breath, the rising and falling. A world complete. The clock mute, turned rudely onto its face. Its deprecations and demands dismissed by guiltless habit. The telephone does not ring. I have been forgotten.

Vonnegut: "We are here on earth to fart around."

Bukowski: "Don't try."

Chandler: "There is nothing to do and I do it."

Those boys are dead.

I cross hands over chest, exhale, smile. The rich darkness. The rain.

If Not Now . . . ?

The days-old baguette requires two hands and some muscle to twist apart, and, in the struggle, an edge of crust stabs my knuckle and draws blood. Good. I am always for a bloodletting, especially one inflicted in the service of a kind act. As I toss the last jagged shapes of bread into the yard for the birds and squirrels, a family of chickadees arrives at the feeder in sudden and furious swoop, takes turns darting to the seed holes, exchanging quick, two-note whistles. I count four birds, but I'm not certain.

Today is the celebration of Martin Luther King, Jr., locally known as the last day of our holiday break between semesters. The dream's over. Tomorrow afternoon I will have two workshops of new poetry students, thirty total, to learn their names and think of something to tell them. This morning, though, a few fat snowflakes drift about, and, thank the lord, it is cold again after many temperate and rainy days. Cold, too, is good. Cold brooks no nonsense, such as my dour and tiresome mood this solitary month. And the dog loves the cold. Lucy is happy and frisky by nature, but when it gets cold, when the snow begins, watch out. I've already survived one spirited pounce. I trust her instincts.

Now a young buck, his winter coat dark, stands in the drive eyeing me. His horns are small but clearly discernible from a distance. Perhaps six inches in length. He watches a moment, then takes his time dissolving into the woods. Today's a last opportunity for quiet. If the ground's still soft enough, I've a bag of crocus bulbs I intend to plant along the stepping stones. Contrary to opinion, I don't believe it's too late.

January Silence

These January days don't lend themselves to words, either written or spoken. I tire of fretting over this, of forcing the issue of communication, of story, of charm. God forbid, of insight. The winter dormancy, the shortened hours of light. A contemplative quiet, a contained interiority. Cautious movement of the body. For the long nights, novels are helpful. Whether I've always been thus, or this is something new, I can't determine. Though I believe there is a kind of sense to it, this waiting. A relief that the future is behind us. See there? Language games. Enough. Much better a reprieve of silence. I am astonished by the résumé of all I no longer desire.

Difficult for my wife, though. She is tireless in efforts to engage me, in her buoyancy. She's pretty as she talks. I am grateful for her patience and pleased to listen, but when the pause comes indicating the time for my response, no fair words arrive.

A Winter Philosophy . . .

. . . of split beef shanks, heavy of marrow bone and white fat, dusted in flour and seared in olive oil in your Dutch oven. Remove. Brown the diced onions and rough-chopped garlic, lots of garlic, a treatise of garlic, then deglaze with a generous pour of red wine, the rest of the bottle in generous proposition. Stir in the beef stock, tomato paste, *bouquet garni* of thyme and rosemary knotted by your own hand, bay leaf, and secret spoonfuls of molasses for umami, adobo for fire. It's your life, and you live it once. Generous grinds of pepper and salt. Taste. Trust the path you've chosen, your sure premise. Return shanks to pot, bring to a boil.

Braise in the oven at a low temperature for three hours. That is, start early, and be patient. Anticipation is itself a pleasure. The wheel of the cold day turns. An inference of bare trees. A solitary cardinal at the feeder. A childhood memory. The bemusing contradiction of whom you have become. The good smells warming the house. Your shared and pleasant hunger. These, the further arguments. An hour before dinner, the early night already descended, add the parsnips, a single sliced carrot, more onion, and return again to the oven. Patience. You are close now. Twenty minutes. Stir in the rinsed white beans, lovely pebbles of cannellini.

You know the rest. Make your case. Bowls and napkins, spoons, warm loaf of bread. The candles lit, the summons that the moment has arrived. Stew in the center of the table, and with a flourish the lid lifted, a conclusion of steam, of rich fragrance, of feast, of hearty reckoning, as full an understanding as you are ever likely to know.

A Simple Moment

Sometimes, just sitting still on the porch swing, dog at your feet, Sunday afternoon and the house to yourself. Say February has begun, two yellow crocuses just bloomed today, one either side of stepping stones. The temperature a balmy 72°F. For once, don't fret the future. The war will resume soon enough, the field taken or lost soon enough. Loose yourself from regret, from worry. Listen: your friend the red-bellied woodpecker, *chuck-chuck*ing invisibly among the trees, wary of approach. He arrives anyway, displaying nicely on a branch. Look up from your book. Slowly, slowly, raise hands. For today, the smaller binoculars, not the monsters, medium magnification but good enough, adequate depth, effortless focusing, sighting in the lenses so easy a child could conquer it. No forensics, not now, no geeky notes or sketches, no expectations, no pride of patience or reward. Just witnessing the alert black eye, the anxious pivoting head and red crown, the black and white striped wings and back. Then the leap to the swaying perch of the feeder, glossy seed collected in slender black beak, and clinging again to the cedar trunk to crack the sweet reward. What a beautiful little creature. Absurd, really, this warmth that forecasts our devastation, this lengthening afternoon light, this quiet joy so unexpected and simply delivered, to be neither held nor contained.

Actual Winter Morning

Lucy straining the leash, giddy with her nose in the dusting of snow, my hands marvelously cold inside my gloves, the wooden slats of our neighbor's unfinished fence capped with white, and not a car or soul in sight as the three of us approach the creek muscled and frothing from a week's rain. The cedars picturesque in their icy shawls, a Bob Ross landscape come to life. How ridiculous and transparent is happiness, how sudden and unapologetic. The dark mood receded, my obsession with the losses of the next years not dispelled, but suspended, abstracted. The losses will wait. I've believed for a long while that humans are foolishly simple animals, not nearly the subtle and intricate nobility we care to imagine. The muddy ground sucking at my new boots, a few fat, cottony flakes in our faces for effect, the sharp call of the unseen kingfisher over the tumultuous green water on its course. There's Claudia. There's Lucy. Here am I. Legs working. Heart working. Breath steady. Eyes to see. Lips to speak. Ears to listen. This instant of eternity. Alive. Alive. Alive.

Winter Bounty

A metronome of snowmelt from the gutter spouts and we are out into the morning. First, to the Feed Supply where Nina has the good news of a dozen eggs reserved for us, a coup. Her chickens have begun to lay, out of season, no explanation tendered by the birds. Nina's eggs always in demand, commonly acknowledged as the best in the county, checkerboard of white, tan, and pastel green artfully arranged in her signature square carton, worthy of photo or canvas. Possibly, she'll have another dozen for us next week.

Then into town, where early on winter Saturdays remnants of the summer market squeeze into the Hamery, an institution for fifty years. On the drive in, passenger observing the felled landscape, I feel ill-tempered, put upon, an inappropriate sourness I know I won't easily shake. Nevertheless: appreciate the ritual, the movement, the community, its goods and our ability to afford them. Get on with it. Inside the cramped space, the aroma of the cured country hams hanging down the staircase is heady, intoxicating. Little Mary, cute as a button, has our 4K Farm greenhouse order bagged, tagged, and ready: panisse, one (picked by her especially for me, and, I am informed, my favorite lettuce); baby romaine, one; leeks, one; garlic scallions, one; gargantuan parsley, one. No rosemary. And no thyme—they rooted it.

Nina's mother-in-law, Mimi, with her loaves and jams and soaps, is absent, but Judy of Conway Farms, a.k.a. the Lamb Lady, is here with our special order: her last four shoulder roasts. Pricey, but as flavorful as any lamb we've ever eaten. She'll take a check. Her husband has stage four cancer and she's getting out of the business. This is her last Hamery visit as a producer. As a surprise, she has brought me three hearts and fourteen small tongues, her entire stash of the latter, a bulky bagful. A gift, honestly, requiring some forbearance. Claudia won't touch any of it and the roasts will already challenge our freezer space. But this is the life I've made. How may one refuse a tribute of fourteen lamb tongues at the right price?

Across the street at the Kwik Mart, while Claudia loads the Subaru, I purchase two freshly baked doughnuts—a glazed chocolate cake and an old-fashioned with maple icing, of course, the doughnut connoisseur's obvious selections—to go with the morning paper and the deferred pleasure of the first cup of coffee. We hightail it for home, as the saying goes, where Lucy awaits. We won't go out the rest of the day, or tomorrow. My ill temper remains, but what the hell. Don't indulge, don't exaggerate. Unpack the haul and practice some gratitude. Make the coffee.

Suicide

Rumor later had it he shot himself in the head in his car in a supermarket parking lot, perhaps Walmart. Details were sketchy, cyber-whispers. Suicide makes people uncomfortable. At the time, all I had for deciphering was a terse email that he'd killed himself, a memorial service to be held in Tennessee that weekend. As I was spending the summer in a cabin near the nonexistent town of Dyea, Alaska, once a bustling port for Gold Rush stampeders, now just trees and paths and an occasional overgrown cellar or foundation stone, pilings like rotted teeth in the slough, I would not be in attendance.

The news surprised and irritated me. Two years earlier, I had been badgered into directing his master's thesis—original poems and an accompanying essay on aesthetics—by a colleague. He was an older student, fortyish, perennially disheveled and rambling—which I hardly remarked at the time—always enthusiastic about poetic process. I didn't pry, but he gave the impression of someone energized by a fresh start. After the thesis defense, I'd gotten him into a fledging MFA program two hours away that a friend had begun. It seemed a good and happy and fortuitous fit. (Only after the fact, having coffee with said friend, who hadn't heard of the death until then, did I learn that my former student had routinely arrived to class—when he attended at all—reeking of booze, had increasingly missed his own classes, and had departed after a single semester. All news to me. Had I been so blind?)

My immediate anger at the suicide caught me off guard, and I was further annoyed that the announcement, stoked by my response, had interrupted my own writing. A selfish distraction from beyond the grave. I gave up on the morning and followed golden retriever Mya—one of three dogs on the property, and the goofiest, always ready for action—down to the West Creek (an Alaska-sized misnomer, as the "creek" was often a frothing river).

Mya never tired of loping into the frigid water to chase sticks she didn't recover, then clambering back to shore a tangled and dripping mess. It occurred to me that my departed student would frolic with no more dogs, study no more rivers, never fear the sudden emergence of bear from the shadows of spruce and cottonwood. Served him right.

The next day, I wrote an impressively crude, derisive, and unpublishable poem addressing his pompous stupidity, agreeably pompous myself. Regarding this poem, I remain neither apologetic nor mollified. The following month, an increasingly isolated time from human company, unfolded slowly for me. Highs and lows. I never tired of the brutal and magnificent landscape—a continually humbling lesson of scale—splitting logs for the woodstove, stealing eggs from the chickens, of the whole corny frontiersman narrative.

A sidebar: My colleague, who'd convinced me to undertake the thesis, had died, suddenly, late the previous summer, in his mid-sixties. He went unexpectedly into the hospital on a Saturday evening and was dead on Tuesday, just before the start of fall classes. "Madame, all stories, if continued far enough, end in death, and no true storyteller would keep that from you." Nearly three years have passed since that moment in the car in the Walmart parking lot. An act signifying what? In pursuit of what last conceit? A presumed courage? A story I will not attempt to its conclusion. Not today.

Flash Memoir Contest

What is Flash Memoir? It is a story of 750 words or less that has a protagonist, a conflict, a setting, excellent use of language, and an ending that we didn't predict when we read the first line. We enjoy stories with a discovery, complex characters, lovely language, and a tone that rings true. There is no formula for success, but a protagonist we care about, a distinctive voice, and a clear impact on the reader all matter. Setting helps. So does conflict and resolution.

—"Writer Advice"

Three days passed. Three banished days never again to exist, each hunted by the night of its reckoning. Within that night's silence, the skirmish of more ghosts than I could count, their indistinguishable guise of jealousy and regret. During this period, no one was ruined, no one saved. Nothing sworn nor betrayed. The world we kept as mute as our skills allowed. Wife and dog in bed, I stood staring into the sky, considering the cipher of its dark origin. The full hunger moon, arrived as predicted, was truly lovely, distinct, obtuse with light. More complex was the same sphere two nights after—diminished, impacted from above, signaling from scurried tendrils of cloud. Humbled moon. Ravaged moon. Moon entreating for witness, as moons will. In short, a damned excellent moon for our protagonist's purpose. Don't you care? The next night, all ceded to blackness—conflicted or resolved, either way an ending we should have seen coming. Or a beginning. I can never tell which. Discovery is an elusive enjoyment. There's no formula. But, believe me, setting helps.

My Father's Breakfast

Daylight by now, pickup loaded with the day's lumber, nail boxes and belts, handmade wooden sawhorses hacked badly in the saddle. Skilsaw—indispensable—ruler, knife-sharpened flat pencil for behind the ear, hammers, drills, chalk line, level. Dad sitting at the table, clean T-shirt and work jeans, loosened boots, Mom frying eggs in bacon fat scooped from a Folgers tin. Biscuits, peppered gravy, a river of bitter coffee. Speaking softly into the early silence, any quarrel of the night delayed, dismissed, forgotten. No hurry now—the quiet suspension, the cool morning. Always forecast of a cold pissing rain, or brutalizing heat, or once in a blue moon a pleasant day. Doesn't matter. Would any of the crew bother to show? Either way. When the job is there, he goes. Maybe a last salted biscuit with butter and sorghum, one more lousy cup. On a rare day I, youngest by a decade, might yawn into the kitchen, warranting a joke re my interrupted "beauty sleep," the pinch of a fat cheek.

Then it was time. Mom refilling the Stanley steel thermos— filled earlier with boiling water—with a second pot of coffee, sandwiches in the cooler, jug of ice water. Boot laces tightened and knotted, stained Porter Paints cap on head, and Dad smiling, wistfully perhaps, willing weary bones to get up and get on with it. All those years, those decades, day after fucking day, until the body announced it was finished. And did I mention all three of his boys would be going to college? No discussion or debate on that subject, ever.

Toohey's Boy

Second grade, the long trek home from John J. Audubon Elementary. Why was I the chosen victim for their threats and taunts? Who knows? Thick eyeglasses, fat kid in fat kid's clothes, a couple years younger. Or the reason of no reason at all. The gauntlet every afternoon was hell, the real education. Mike, my oldest brother, planning to leap from behind a tree in intervention, laughably screwed the play. Reading or snoozing, he didn't even see us pass. That trip a misery of pokes, pushes, scattered books and papers, announcements of the sorry beating I was very soon to take, all the way to my block.

Then the Saturday, like a frightful dream, I saw the chief brute being marched down our street and toward the house. I tried invisibility, but Dad ushered me to the front door. The punk's dad, towering behind him, fists clenched on the bony shoulders, growled, "You got something you want to say?" Eternity passed. My father looming behind me. The punk's father slapped his neck. Eyes lowered, half his normal size, he mumbled a perfunctory "sorry," "we didn't' mean nuthin'," et cetera. Then he walked away, a punk defeated. I later learned that, after my brother botched it, Dad had visited Toohey's Auto Service to remind the proprietor, quote, "Toohey, I kicked your ass when we were kids and I can kick your ass now."

What do we take from this humorous, if ambivalent, lesson, a championed moment of family lore? Hoorah, as far as I was concerned. The good bully prevails! Toohey's boy would be in his mid-fifties today. Is it arrogant to speculate on his years, the generational lessons passed to his own brood? I've hated bullies all my life, all their endless iterations. But looking back nearly a half century at that stupid, violent kid, hair limp in his eyes, staring at ugly sneakers, blank with humiliation and rage, mouthing his fake contrition, I feel almost sorry for the little goon and what was being learned by both of us. Almost.

Art, Lust & Money

An endless February in an endless season. Leap Year into what? If I wore a winter mood in the past, I never noticed. One small gray deer crosses the drive, then another. The day's second hailstorm—dots of ice small as pinheads—drops tepidly from a gray sky, melting away in minutes into the saturated gray earth. Half-hearted harbingers. When was the last hour of clear sky, its taunt of sun and promise? I've a few stories yet to tell, but not today, not today. Today, surrender to the artless. Wait.

Yes, I have again completed thirty unpleasant days without drink (long nights, lots of reading) to prove some inchoate point to myself. This past week I've recommenced the habit (blurry nights, no reading) and learned nothing from that, either. Eighty-three thousand now infected with the virus. A pandemic looms but the scraggly woods of Tennessee seem a safe bet. The stock market burns. In four days, more than a year's salary in flames, and counting. I can't stomach looking at the carnage of the numbers. I feel a detachment, an unreality, an unbecoming self-indulgence that's hard to shake loose. My wife avoids speaking to me. There's an immobility, a sense of suspension, of waiting . . . for what? Elements as simple as light, and warmth? The birds have abandoned the feeder. Even the squirrels desultory. Clearing the crocuses choked with weed seems an insurmountable task. Cheatgrass. Henbit. Shepherd's purse. Conjure-words denuded of power.

That covers art and money, a sample of nature. And the third priority? What, a lust for life? I dread the telephone, the loss it will ring into our lives. Yet what can one do but mechanically answer? "Hello? Hello? Who's there?" Tomorrow is February 29, another wrong thing. But at last some good news—the burial of this gray month. The latest Unprecedented Summer of Recorded Temperature hot on its heels.

Stan Lee, Hugh Hefner

When I saw Mr. Hefner's photo in 2017 above the announcement of his death, for a moment I believed it to be Stan Lee. Maybe that confusion wasn't so peculiar: the lined old face, leathered with sun, of a deity I'd grown up with; the small eyes; the perpetual own-the-world-Cheshire-cat grin. Lee followed the next year. Two nonagenarians dead in LA, two kingdom-builders of fantasy. By the time of their respective deaths, the Hef/Playboy Mansion mythos curiously infantilized on the reality series *The Girls Next Door*; Lee's public persona reduced to wait-for-it cameos in films recycled ad nauseum for a multi-billion-dollar industry of techno-porn righteousness long since sold, plundered, and resold. *Playboy* lost, Marvel won, if anyone's keeping score: pubescent piety over pubescent prurience, a weary totem over taboo, or perhaps vice versa.

But ah, in the '50s and '60s, when these two men were kings . . .

I never met Hefner, unfortunately, but I did have a peculiar, never-explained intersection with Mr. Lee. I'll throw a dart and guess the year was 1976. Buried in *The Comics Buyer's Guide* (a.k.a. *CBG*)—a primitively edited newspaper tabloid chock-full of fan gossip and debate and all manner of merchandise for negotiated purchase (in other words, indispensable reading)—was a crummy-looking, quarter-page ad for a forgettable one-day comic book convention in Indianapolis, hardly worth the hundred-plus-mile drive from Louisville. Except for one tantalizing, dubious element: a crudely-drawn balloon announcing Stan Lee's appearance. My older brother and I were incredulous, but how could we risk it? Lee was a legend, a trickster-god, an elemental and cosmic force. His rare appearance at a major con on either coast was rumored to draw queues the length of city blocks.

Well, True Believer, to this day I wonder about the unlikely circumstances. Old friend? Favor granted or recalled? Family commitment? Or just, what the hell? But there he sat, Stan the Man himself—trademark wide grin, mustache, shaded specs—relaxed at a card table with maybe two dozen of the faithful in line. Lee all smiles and couldn't have been nicer, as if a crappy hotel in central Indiana was the most compelling place in the world for him to be, as he signed my tattered copy of *Spider-Man* #3 ("Can Anything That Lives, [*sic*] Defeat The Mighty Doctor Octopus??") Only one tense moment marred the sublimity. I was squeezed into a Superman T-shirt—why had no adult intercepted this flagrant transgression?—the last thing on my mind as I stood dazzled and dazed in the Presence. Lee stared at the iconic insignia stretched across my gut. His smile dimmed. Even before I intuited the cause, I could feel his eyes narrow behind the darkened lenses. "He's not one of ours," he said simply, accusingly, saying it all, as he pointed a lean finger at my young heart.

Then he laughed.

Choose Your Superpower!

Some say Armageddon by fire, some say by ice. Yadda yadda. Notwithstanding, bursting into flame is not a superpower. Shooting icicles from your palms is not a superpower. Nor, for that matter, is a reddened visor ablaze with laser beams. These are grotesque, pitiable afflictions. Sick puppies. Mastery of magic is also not a superpower, neither is gadgetry, athleticism, elasticity, nor possessing high intelligence (yes, the latter's rarity argues for elevation of its status). X-ray vision? Ugh. Unnatural power to heal oneself (albeit only physically as the mind swirls) is intriguing, especially in days of violence and contagion, but this, too, is more oddity. The core superpowers boil down to three: super strength, flight, and invisibility. Let us consider.

1. *Super strength.* Clearly the thug's universal choice, power of preference for rednecks, hooligans, a dishearteningly large portion of the current electorate, bullies, children, and those lacking subtlety, grace, and imagination. Knocking down that first brick wall might amuse and impress, but by the second leveling it's a yawn. Sure, flipping an ersatz monster truck—one, say, with exhaust customized to roar upon acceleration (making god-awful noise is not a superpower, it's being an asshole; but let's not bring neighbors into this . . .)—toward the moon might gratify, yet even so. Not to be gruesome, but what good is super strength, O Goliath, O dull-witted Colossus of the wide stance, when the flung stone penetrates head, heart, or worse (i.e., balls)? (Super strength is often illogically linked with invincibility. How can the metaphor of the invincible be quantified as a power? A .50 caliber shell exploding human tissue is no abstraction. Super strength, friend, ain't bulletproof. The first gangbanger or righteous yokel with a bump stock and you're dead. Toast. And a suit of titanium armor might be useful in a brawl, but it's a billionaire brat's toy, not—ahem—a superpower.)

2. *Flight*. Granted, this is the romantic option, superficially pleasant to think on, and convenient for short trips. Otherwise, though, what is it but a cheap "high"? Let's be candid. The purpose of the blessing/curse of a superpower is a) notionally, to help "humanity"—i.e., American citizens—and b) to make money. How will an individual's ability to fly enable either of these laudable goals? What? Rent oneself out as pony (i.e., freak) for birthday parties and bar mitzvahs? Start a modest home delivery service? In the margin of either humanitarian service or profit, a degrading bargain. And (okay, speaking of neighbors) how long before that good ole boy blows you out of the sky with a lucky potshot? *Got dat flyin' focker!* Yes, taking wing is the liberal preference, no-brainer for Lefties, tree huggers, Icarus chumps, the overeducated, and those who miss their mamas. Good luck. Enjoy your flight.

3. *Invisibility*. Younger, I considered this the most cynical and insidious superpower. That's because it is! It's also the smart choice for today's world. Let us not distract ourselves with some petty rhubarb regarding, say, whether clothing will also transform to the unseen or whether you must return always naked to the visible. Nor unduly stress over how one gets past the proverbial drawbridge, over the gate, through the guards. We'll learn the science of modesty, the skillset of deception, as we go. And think bigger, so much bigger, than petty larcenies and ho-hum voyeurism. Consider instead those demented villains, the Super Rich, feverish in their plush installations, scheming at their desks. There are a few clubhouse rendezvous that never happened that I'd like to attend, some nonexistent conference calls to eavesdrop, my presence nothing more than a breeze unnoticed, hint of shadow just as quickly gone, imperceptible fly on the blood-stained wall. Initially, of course, invisibility's huge rewards will be for me alone. First things first. But then, humanity—on my word as a hero—for *you*!

IV: SPRING

virus weeding; the new cruel month; Samuel Pepys; panic baking; masks; Ramadan; Alamo; death game; Frank Sinatra dead in Provence; goat brain curry

Advice on Weeding in Face of a Virus Pandemic and Plummeting World Markets

for Chauncey Gardiner

Any month can be a cruel month. Perhaps the sure future of two weeks ago lies in ruin. In the garden, you live season by season. If you prayed for March to arrive, its early blooms, then your prayer has been answered. The garden gone to seed must be tended. Perhaps this is not your fault, perhaps no one's, but whose responsibility now if not yours? The abandoned garden cannot be reclaimed in a day. Get on your knees beside the pathway. Give your hands to the dirt. Last year's hyacinths are thin in flower, but flagrant, deeply violet, deeply blue. Weeding demands judgment, force mediated with care. You must not destroy the beauty you dedicated to reveal. Some choices are easy. The small blue bells of the grape hyacinth, spreading each year in undaunted clumps. Consider the tiny white stars-of-Bethlehem: intrusions, or to be granted their fragile existence? Moment by moment, the gardener must decide. To root or extract. To nurture or banish. Take your time. Stay your course. More hard weather is forecast, but the instant is bright and clear and the breeze pleasant. The clusters of crocuses you planted only a month ago, absurdly, disregarding all instruction, all science of their germination? Well, see green tendrils churning soil, the white bulb of a first flower enclosing its golden stamen. The garden will break your heart every time, but all is not lost. Move from stone to stone, bent to your labor. Belief is not required. Hope is not required. Clear one modest space of all but what belongs. To work in the garden is an act of faith. Your task will not be finished in a day. It will never be finished. Strive only for the simple achievement of the hour, noticed by no one. A revelation of space, balance, and form in a cosmos of inches. Restoration is reverence. The earth listens. So many elements the gardener cannot control, only a fool would continue. Submit to this humbling fate. Control is illusion, and that, too, is a gift. If you're not careful, you may look up into the open sky and feel joy.

Clearwater

Hours after that decision . . . the Clearwater City Council held their emergency meeting that ultimately ended in the vote to close Clearwater Beach.
—March 19, 2020

Today is my father's eighty-eighth birthday, and, for reasons related to the COVID-19 crisis, I will not see him. We spoke twice this morning, trading our habitual silly stories and premonitions. He sounded rough-voiced, only a bit dispirited. But I will not see him or my mother, the latter laid low by a lingering and ominous cold. Travel suddenly seems a remnant of distant, naïve times. Thursday is the first day of spring, so the calendar believes, and it promises to be a deadly one of great cost and consternation.

Instead, I conjure the Spring Breaks of my childhood, when the family would load up the cavernous trunk of the Buick and go out for dinner (perhaps at The Ponderosa or Cow Palace). Afterward, Dad would drive all night for Florida, he and Mom in the front, we three boys restlessly dozing and intertwined in the back. (In later years, my older brothers would sometimes feign some other commitment, but, more often than not, a last-minute revision of schedule and hankering for the ocean got them in the car.)

I-65 to Nashville, I-24 to Chattanooga, picking up I-71 and through Atlanta, to Macon and onward south. With luck, ten hours from Louisville to the Florida border, then another four hours to Clearwater (a bit longer if after Lake City we veered right on US-47 to intersect with the scenic US-98 toll road down). Crossing the state line just as the sun rose was the symbolic tipping point of arrival. Soon, a first sighting of palm trees in the pink sky. Not long after, we'd stop at Huddle House for breakfast. Clambering out stiff and yawning into the warm, salty morning, that thick Florida air. Plenty of time now to make our motel by midday.

Then, a week together, a hot-footed three-block walk to the beach. At low tide, hunting shells and stranded surprises: starfish, jellyfish, snarls of seaweed. Pelicans and gulls. Pods of dolphins, the requisite shark joke regarding fins. Runs of mackerel. Red skin, blisters. Fried fish and hush puppies and sweet tea. Towels always damp, the smell and smear of lotion, sand anywhere sand could get. AC unit dripping, laboring away to cool the room. I sit here and it returns to me. A Clearwater Beach you wouldn't recognize now. And somewhere in that history, the last year we went.

(March 16, 2020)

Note to Samuel Pepys

16 August 1665: But, Lord! how sad a sight it is to see the streets empty of people, and very few upon the 'Change. Jealous of every door that one sees shut up, lest it should be the plague; and about us two shops in three, if not more, generally shut up.

* * *

31 August 1665: I have never lived so merrily (besides that I never got so much) as I have done this plague time.
—*Diary of Samuel Pepys*

21 March 2020. Yes, I too have the public indignities against me to record, some few adventures of gastronomy and drink, affairs of household, heart, and illicit desire, the private gossip and paltry victories that, sadly, sustain and define a man. The daily conceits. Yes, I write them down. But how your chronicled decade pales against our mere half a year. Your Great Fire? We've a continent consumed in conflagration. Another, by locusts whose numbers and hunger exceed Biblical imagination. Your Great Plague? We've a pandemic eruption, an End of Days still in its infancy: 303,433 infections, 12,964 deaths, betting odds reported in real time. What could you know of "flattening the curve," of fortunes vanished in seconds, of the sure future of weeks ago now a laughable haze? Inhalation of calamity, exhalation of despair. The peace of helplessness. That's how we roll now, Sam.

Your vaunted Second Dutch War? A skirmish. Your hapless and dissembling leaders? Let's not even speak of it. I've no cause to embarrass you, to laugh at the expense of your naïveté. It's not your fault, my advantage of four hundred years. You did your best with events unfolding before you. Showed us the way. Turned a nice profit. Perhaps you did possess a sensibility for our age, if no plausible context to believe in it. *Who could have seen this coming?*, the king announces rhetorically. Our Greatness, it seems, knows no bounds. If, again among us and so compelled, you lowered pen to parchment, you might just feel all thoughts overwhelmed. As I have written these few, another 908 are reported infected, twenty-three more dead. As if the words themselves were somehow to blame. So let us stop. More tomorrow.

In Time of Crisis and Quarantine, the Insistence of Small Things

I get lucky, steal two hours between storms to mow a section of the ragged spring lawn, a rebuking mess with weed, wild onion, and shaggy clump. I've even spare minutes to get fussy, trim along the foundation and the garden's woolly edge. A little disorder temporarily put right. What I can contribute before the rains, which seem they will never stop, rains that have moved far beyond metaphor for our helpless gloom to merely embellish the world's dark and tallied announcements, return to banish me to our home transformed to comfortable prison. My wife, meanwhile, attacks her writing room with a fastidious fury. Organizing files, straightening books, polishing shelves and frames, dust rag and vacuum. She soaks the globes of the miniature oil lamps in soapy water. Wipes clean the boots of the Russian doll in mink cap I brought her from St. Petersburg, from a different life.

Small things to stave off the hand that trembles on its own, then stops. The blade of argument flashed over nothing. The sudden intake of breath, a panicked heart. It's a jumble. A mess of fragments. Forgive me. The pressed button on the radio and the news topping each unforeseeable hour. The bruising isolation of intimacy, of disembodiment. On and on. Nothing remains to ironize. Satire has a sour taste. To pause. To exhale. Unclench the hand. To strive to be patient and kind. Before the sky closes in again, I look across the manicured square of green, its neat edges. It is glowing. Further, our scraggly forsythias have never looked so effusive, so beautiful, have never, I believe, tried so hard. I cheer them on in gratitude. Yellow has no desire for subtlety. Yellow just wants to be happy. Fragments. Shadows. Fear.

When, sweaty and aching from my work, I reenter the house, I smell the pungent lemon polish, see the dusting cloth crumbled on the carpet like—again, forgive me—vanquished flag or soiled shroud of the dead. What I mean to say is, the polish smells clean and good. Insistent. A drum of thunder in the sky. However many hours remaining before today is done.

Good Friday, Worldwide Death Toll
from Pandemic Surpasses 100,000

A number that no citizen of reasonable cynicism believes anywhere near the unfathomable reality. The next morning the sun rises, a pure and cleansing April brightness. I sit on the front stoop, mesmerized by warm light. Lucy lies panting in the garden. We are, ostensibly, waiting for my wife's return from the outside with vegetables, bread, the numbing daily headlines, whatever she finds. In the meantime, I am reading from a book of poetry. Why not? The latest numbers of the dead and ill will arrive soon enough. This is her first time out in over a week, first venture in a homemade mask. It is her turn. The yard is freshly trimmed and radiant. Our dogwood sapling blooms, unapologetically pink. The lilac opens as well, though the blowsy sweetness of what it once was has thinned in recent years to a scraggly truth. Even our maddening neighbors are oddly quiet this morning, during the pause between the death and the rebirth. Wrens and finches sing their praise. The sun on my face and arms is magnificent, and it is as if for a moment the life we imagined, that we nearly convinced ourselves was ours by no other right than grace and luck, a myth of good works, that such a life existed, and we lived it.

Panic Baking at the End of the World:
Upside-Down Cake with Rum and Fresh Pineapple

Let us go to our fate with a fête of sweet fat, sugar, and salt. Of celebration on the tongue and nostalgia in the heart. Of knives, alchemy, and heat. Here is our recipe.

1. Take the last pineapple from Costa Rica and, with calming strokes, skin and core the fruit with the widest blade, separate armor from tender flesh. Cut into the thick wedges you will need to form your mosaic.
2. Take the last eggs and rich butter from the local farmer, purchased in an open field at the last Saturday market. Take a careful measure of the last artisan flour. Take the final small pleasures of the earth we came to believe we deserved.
3. Take the last cups of brown and white sugar, the last teaspoons of sea salt and pungent vanilla. The last tart buttermilk.
4. Take the last bottle of white Bacardi capped in Puerto Rico and break the seal. Be generous with your pour.
5. This is a modest cake, a cake of international devotions, cake of diaspora, cake of the world's last harvest, of dance, of slaughter, of savory and sweet, of tears and joy and fear and praise, sacrament and failure, of recognition too late.
6. A cake of layers. The soft butter spread thick in the pan. The sprinkling of the dark sugar, and nestled into it our arrangement of the succulent yellow fruit. Take your time. Create a tight pattern, one that pleases, a surface patchwork yet nearly whole. Spoon over with the unctuous batter until all is covered.
7. On this last night, as the power wanes, bake in a last hot oven until firm and golden and too beautiful to now exist. Remove with care.

That maddening fragrance overwhelming the house. My god. Close your eyes. Breathe. Everything we lived for and thought would last forever. Let it cool. Let it cool. Then invert. You see? Right side up, after all. As it was meant to be. No need for panic. And a last slice for each of us, on our prettiest dishes, by candle-light on this very special night.

Birthday Sonata

I am always at a loss to know how much to believe
of my own stories.
                    —Washington Irving

April has arrived, along with the near-end of our third week of self-quarantine, and my birthday as well, which I share with Washington Irving and Marlon Brando. If you confuse us, just remember that I am the one, for the moment, still breathing. But for how long? My dad couldn't wait so called yesterday to let his "baby boy" know, again, that today I would be the same age as my grandfather when he died of a stroke. Mom called first thing this morning, with a glee almost equaling the old man's, to remind me of "the hell" I put her through the day I was born. Ha. And fair enough. Their governor has closed the border between our states.

I spent the afternoon cutting the lawn—numbing, mindless labor with a controlled and pretty result. My hands are still shaking from the weed whacker as I struggle to type. That thing is a bear, but priceless for release of stress, a cheap whirring thrill of violence. The unambiguous leveling of the unwanted. Yard work and gardening are ideal for these times, if the weather's good, and today was sunny, unnaturally warm. Under the circumstances, I'll take it. We've had some bad losses in the garden, too, but allow me to report one success. The dogwood I planted five years ago—a bare stick—is flowering for the first time. Nearly six feet tall, nicely shaped, trunk thick as a half dollar, flowers pink as advertised. A modest miracle. In the bluebird box, a couple has moved in, handsome and industrious. Everyone, experts and otherwise, agree we face a dire month, that the worst is yet to come. That we must remain in isolation and brace ourselves.

My wife retrieved a small lamb roast from the back of the freezer. The stashes of gin and wine are, for now, holding. The dog daydreams of a time when the world of the house was sometimes all her own but is otherwise tolerant. I sent a fat donation to World Central Kitchen (god bless Saint José Andrés) so can ignore my soul for the rest of the day. Ignore the telephone as well, and ruminate over my new mantra for the year. "Fifty-five, still alive." "Fifty-five, why survive?" Not good enough.

"Name and address withheld"

All right, I confess—although I'm uncertain of the statute of limitations, these accusatory days, for having published a letter in *Penthouse* "Forum." I'm hoping that more than three decades will suffice. (Just in case, I'm offering insufficient detail for the evidence to be too easily exhumed and entered against me.) By the cover date, my second year of graduate school, probably composed for no worthier reason than I'd just finished writing (or was assiduously avoiding writing) a long essay for, say, Victorian Novel Seminar or some such.

After a search, I found the magazine at the bottom of a yellowed pile and read the letter. Shameful, amateurish, but a fair compilation of the crude detail, cringing euphemism, and flat-footed farce that constituted the hallmarks of the genre. "Forum" letters were famously hyperbolic, laughable fantasies, "discreetly" anonymous and transparent (surely?) even to the dimmest pubescent reader. That was part of the "fun," if fun it was. Anyway, imagine our setting: a *corrida* in Mexico City, fateful tryst at the animal cages beneath the event, our narrator thinking nostalgically of the climactic moment with his inamorata, the sultry and willing Rosita. "We could hear the crowd shouting '*Toro! Toro!*' and Rosita echoed the chant. '*Toro!*' she cried. '*Más! Más!*' She was looking at the bulls as I continued to . . ." And so forth. No belles lettres, but the young author has the required clichés accounted for. There is one amusing moment, late in this tedious missive, when the narrator deadpans, "Her English was getting better." And it was!

So, I was a minor celebrity that week to the couple of guys in our shared office I discreetly showed the piece, though even then it was an embarrassment. At its peak, *Penthouse* had a circulation exceeding five million, and the notorious "Forum" was its most popular column. It is not lost on me the . . . not irony . . . the perfect *absurdity* that this will remain, by a colossal margin, the most widely read piece I will ever write, although not perhaps by my typical demographic. The letter ends with a timeless trope: "My friends won't believe me, and I guess you'll have trouble believing me, too. But it happened, and I look forward to returning to Mexico." Indeed!

Incidentally, two years later Ohio State picked up the tab to send me to Cuernavaca to complete my foreign language requirements for the PhD, a semester during which I spent several weekends in Mexico City. Nothing to report, dear reader. Absolutely *nada*.

Mask

He has changed himself into something awful,
only by hiding his face.
—Nathaniel Hawthorne

My first time, so I ponder the wardrobe: the black bandanna crossed with human skulls seems gauche, the stiff red too riddled with bank-robber cliché. I select a soft kerchief of blue, decorated with paisley and diamonds within concentric squares. Fold diagonally, then double, then over the nose and mouth and tied snug at the base of the neck.

Walking from the car I am a self-conscious fool, but as I enter, into the charged moment of contact, I realize the profound effect of my conversion. The unmasked outnumber us still, but our numbers grow every day. I spread my wife's wishlist beside my own in the basket, and as I join the fray feel transformed, strangely out of body and yet acutely contained within myself. Distanced. Focused. Purposeful. We the masked offer no eye contact, no jokes of the sickness, move efficiently aisle to aisle, touching only our selected goods. The unmasked continue to talk among themselves, some standing still as if confused. Standing too close, as if congregation were courage. I do not judge. I am *other*.

I get lucky. Apples of choice, green bananas, carrots. My wife's favorite tea back in stock. My breath hot and suffocating in my face. No chicken, but a single rib roast on display. I rush forward, incredulous, cost irrelevant, cradle it into the cart for Easter. It is mine. When I look down the desolate paper and toiletries lane, ground zero, there, inexplicable on the barren shelves, are a half dozen packages of my preferred paper towels. A mirage. When I wheel closer, the towels remain, existent for purchase, and I claim two packages. A young woman has turned into the aisle behind me, and, witnessing the rows of naked shelving, exhales an overly loud, "Are you kidding me?" She stops. Her head begins to swivel.

"No." Sotto voce. "*No. No. No.*" She is near a breaking point, but I offer no solace, no companionable comment, nor point out the remaining rolls of towels. She, the unmasked, must endure on her own.

No milk, no butter. I find insect repellent, toothpaste. At home, we have a surplus of toilet paper, coffee, local eggs, none of it acquired without price. To the checker I nod, say nothing, hear the animal breath alive in my nostrils. Touch the keypad with a Q-tip. Already, the alien become routine, the unthinkable merely common sense. Outside, a day seeming fair. I push the cart along, careful to keep my hands on its disinfected handle. Pull the mask down and gulp clear air, contagious or not, no more or no less human.

Alamo

March 6, 2020. Was it coincidence I was there among the tourists, no masks, no distance between us? Nostalgia. The reenactors in leather brogans, trousers, and waistcoats, their flintlocks and dragoon swords polished for display. The conference I had flown in for had not been its typical schmoozing affair. Empty aisles of the cavernous hall and announcements of canceled events slanted the weekend toward the surreal. From the soft bed of my B&B, the unwatchable news, watched each evening. I knew I would never attend the organization again, but that was my private story, lost and silenced in the greater one looming. I found a bench beside a fountain in the quietest corner of the gardens, between the cannons and the exhibit hall, next to a marvelous live oak more than a century old. We crowded together, celebrating the courage of defeat. William Travis shot and killed early, defending the east wall. James Bowie, feverish in his bed, pierced by bayonet. After the exterior had fallen, Davie Crockett defending to death the Mission's church. They had withstood two charges of Santa Anna's troops that bleak, breaking dawn. The third vanquished them all. The shaded spot by the fountain was pleasant, and I held the bench for a while, not anxious to surrender it. I was alone, considering my own small narrative among all the others, relieved to be done with preening and self-promotion. In the morning, my hired car would deliver me to a deserted airport. Hours in flux soon to become the norm.

Anyway, that was the week, that handful of days at the beginning of March, our lives strangely fluid yet so much already still and determined, stark future imminent, when we knew what was coming but couldn't fathom it, couldn't stop it, couldn't believe in other than the victory of our resistance. That those forces—invisible, that had already arrived—would overwhelm us.

The Solace of Birding During a Pandemic

bird by bird I've come to know the world . . .
—Neruda

Yes, we must parole ourselves with a short hike to the creek when we require the rattling welcome of kingfisher, a daggered arrow low over the surface; the single heron risen on wide, languid wings at our approach; geese nonchalantly distancing over shallow rapids.

Otherwise, I need merely to wait on the porch swing each isolated hour as they come to the feeder, our feathered visitors. Quick, curious, hungry, they arrive in this clement weather. Cardinal and titmouse, jay and wren, robin, chickadee, downy woodpecker and larger red-bellieds, a lovely couple, whose insistent *churrr* summons me from the jail of our home. The goldfinch in his lemony summer glow a fine confidant. The mated bluebirds, handsome and hardworking, who attack the yard in the evening to feed their wide-mouthed brood. A lone and leisurely turkey hen.

And yesterday, sitting with a book on the back deck, our most private spot, the western light slicing through branches, another calendar day of our containment nearly crossed out, I sensed movement, a great peripheral shape from trunk to trunk, heard the announcing *cuk cuk cuk cuk* and, yes!, there in sudden full view the enormous pileated woodpecker, grail of local birding, augury sighted a dozen times in two decades. The zigzagging black and white of face and neck, the full and thrilling red crest. It clung nearby for several seconds. The visitation mine alone, this news from the feral world, beyond the illness and depredations of our own, that its wild beauty still existed, that it wished me hope.

Then it was gone.

The Solace of the Future

That a thirty-kilometer "exclusion zone" surrounding Chernobyl is now an Eden abundant with buffalo and deer, white-tailed eagles, robust packs of gray wolves, is a satisfying irony. In the weeks since our national parks shut, black bears are said to have quadrupled in appearance in Yosemite, are walking openly down deserted roads. Coyotes and bobcats explore empty cabins. Explained one park ranger, the animals are "having a party." And don't they deserve it! After thirteen years of ignoring their keepers' prodding, the pandas Ying Ying and Le Le have mated in Hong Kong's closed Ocean Park Zoo. From India to Costa Rica, nesting sea turtles have returned to dark and empty beaches. With factories shuttered, cars in garages, planes on the ground, nitrogen and carbon dioxide emissions have plummeted almost overnight "more dramatically than ever seen." Blue skies are reported in Detroit, Chicago, Rome, even, to the amazement of all, Beijing.

Today is, coincidentally, the fiftieth anniversary of Earth Day, founded by the well-named Gaylord Nelson. We are all watching through our windows, lamenting so much irrecoverable, acknowledging what splendor remains. Sure, in no time the engines of industry will rev, the wheels of commerce roll with a giddy carnage. "Revenge pollution," I've heard it called. So be it. Let us rush on in full disregard, on to our deserved end. Jeffers' poems, long since erased from the anthologies, come pleasantly to mind. The implacability of stone. The ferocity of hawk. As far down the coast as its keen eye can see, not a human in sight. Nor one to notice.

Ramadan Begins at Sunset

The Islamic holy month had begun and I was critically low on alcohol with no way to restock. I'd planned ahead, but nevertheless some disciplined math was required to survive. Then it was the final evening in Marrakesh, the final half bottle. I'd taken my last stumble through the maze of the vast medina, slurped a last bowl of *babbouche*—the addictive snail soup—nodded my goodbyes to the cobra charmers on Jemaa el-Fna Square, and with my very last dirhams negotiated a taxi back to the Hôtel Gomassine. (I'd prepaid the car to the airport at dawn.)

The others had departed the day before. The rooftop of the hotel was deserted. Bats lunged in and out the elevated letters of its signage. I sipped my last inches of warm gin. The tangerine sky over the Guéliz district darkened to fire, then to a luminous night. I felt tired, serene. I'd always enjoyed the melancholic hours before leaving a place to which I would never return. The world was mine and had been for a long time.

That was 2019. When you could venture nearly anywhere, intrude on any culture, frolicking and protected, and return home when you chose. Remember those days? How we almost took it all for granted?

I drained the glass.

Coronavirus Deaths in the US Surpass 50,000

—April 26, birthday of John James Audubon

The song of the tanager, to me, sounds like a flow of clear water. A brook. I had never heard or seen them here until the day after Jasper died, fifteen years gone. Since, they visit perhaps annually. A few evenings ago, a bright cool twilight, that distinctive call. The next morning, the rose-red male of this typically shy bird, perched high in a cedar, offers a leisurely sighting through the binoculars, singing all the time. Another day, I am reading a chapter on peregrine falcons when a broad-winged hawk skims low and fast over the roof and disappears into the woods. I overuse the word augury. How about serendipity? Or simply an abiding affection, sustenance for the spirit.

It's been a good week for birding. On my weekly drive into town for groceries, top down, face mask still in my pocket, a meadowlark on an electric line, yellow breast crossed with a stylish black "V." Down at the creek, rarer, a juvenile blue heron, white and thin-necked as an egret, rousted silently from the bank on its long wings. Closer to home, the bluebird chicks in the box are nearly fledged, still hungry.

Mostly, though, the birds come to me. In fair weather, self-quarantine takes the form of watching, of waiting, the birder's prime attributes, and all the usual avian friends arrive. This time of year, the lemon glow of the goldfinch in his spring plumage is a common highlight. The male red-bellied woodpecker swoops in reliably every morning and afternoon, not at all shy in announcing his arrival with a noisy *chuck chuck chuck*. Speaking of raucous, a single blue jay has been a regular, a bright handsome bird I remind myself to appreciate. I don't often see one at the feeder. The mourning dove, meanwhile, strikes a softer note. Two elegant turkey hens peruse the property individually then meet, comely dowagers, to peck at stray sunflower seeds fallen to the ground.

A pair of cowbirds stop by for a day. Magnified, the male is a surprising showstopper: the glossy chocolate-brown head, russet body, dark beak and eye.

No sign, however, of the ruby-throated hummingbird, who should have arrived by now to hover at the blooming columbine. I've been awaiting the demanding squeaks, the darting blurs of its aviation. The absence is a concern. Some migratory delay or worse.

As of this morning, more than 50,000 dead.

Good News Dispatch (with Death Toll)

I love wild things almost to foolishness . . .
—John Clare

Welcome, May! Two worrisome weeks late, by my math, the ruby-throated hummingbirds have at last arrived. Anyway, a single female, her impatient squeak unmistakable. I get the nectar made and cooled—not too sweet so as not to attract wasps—the feeder hung with its squirrel guard, with Vaseline on the hook to discourage ants. Precautions, provisions. For now, they suffice, and she returns throughout the day, darting and hovering, dividing thirst between platform and columbine. To my amazement, a downy woodpecker also arrives to attack the sweet syrup. Unprecedented, how he might, clinging, angle into the miniscule hole.

May Day, and the fledgling bluebirds have left the box—four anxious and hardy chicks—and all morning practiced flights and landings. There is still some learning to do, but they greet their lessons, this first free day, with noisy vigor. We've lost several clutches, to attacking chickadees—horrible, unstoppable event I've witnessed twice—and I suspect to snakes. It's a perilous, predatory existence, so these awkward young are cause for excitement.

"come May / again / white blossom // . . . down / and quickly / fall" (William Carlos Williams)

Meanwhile, two toads, gray and bulbous-eyed, size of my thumb, have moved in beneath a stepping stone, into a generous hole from which they watch me with increasing boldness. A good-looking pair of amphibians, in my opinion. I like their attitude and think of them down in the cool darkness, safe as the world allows.

(May 1, 2020: 62,406 Coronavirus deaths—reported—in the US.)

The Purpose of Birding

*Most of the world's ills come from the human inability
to sit quietly in silence.*
　　　　　　　　　　　　　—Pascal

A bad night and the day it engendered. Stressful day, day of impatience, without peace or reprieve, wasted day of nothing concluded. A day I'd given up on when I stepped onto the porch with drink and book, hoping for a few minutes transported elsewhere. Silly-ass birds the last thing on my mind when I saw the figure hopping in the unkempt lawn. Even as I flashed on the thought of indigo bunting, I knew it wasn't, knew instinctively and immediately, with intake of breath, it was something new that I'd never seen in two decades of caretaking the property. A rarity. A first sighting. In calculated risk, I stepped backward through the door, grabbed binoculars from bench, and cautiously returned. A male blue grosbeak, deep shimmering hue, black eye and blunt black bill. Regal buff wing patches topped with auburn epaulets. A fine and generous bird, or anyway an indifferent one, granting me a long look in the shaggy grass, then full view on an elm branch, and one last perch before disappearing into the woods. Giving me a little opening, a little light, a gift of effortless wild beauty in a day I had wanted finished and forgotten.

Elizabethtown City Cemetery

Harsh and strident notes, often ascending, like killy-killy-killy,
and others that sound like squeaky chattering.
                    —*The Audubon Society Field Guide*

I'd skipped the funeral home, instead driven three hours to
surprise them at the burial site. A guilt-relieving compromise.
The turbulent sky and pelting rain had abated. I circled up into
the hills of markers and monuments. I wasn't too late, after all,
and the masked gravedigger in his truck informed me that the
entourage was behind schedule and also that they'd have to stop
down the way. The hole was trying to collapse. My own face
mask lay in the passenger seat. I parked out of view, hiked up
to the mound of dirt, considered a few flat, eroded stones, dates
and vaguely familiar names. I was hoping to be back on the road
within an hour and, pedal to the metal, home in time for dinner.

Perched clumsily on a low stone wall, I read an article on the
dying art of Palermo puppet theater, *Teatro dei Pupi*, a family's
five generations of *pupari* coming to an end. An eastern kingbird,
animated, leapt from stone to stone. In flight, the white tips of
its black tail feathers fanned attractively. Stiff from the drive, I
stood and followed until the bird swooped out of sight. Down the
hill, a hearse and three cars had arrived. A powder-blue coffin on
a stand. A handful of folks, none of whom I knew: pudgy man in
coat and tie, tiny old lady, three or four others milling about. The
digger had assured me this was the only burial. I was in the right
place. Well, perhaps a few strangers had tagged along. It was a
beautiful day now, cool clear sky, wisps of high cloud, the languor
of late afternoon, and I'd been cheered by the kingbird.

I started over the lush grass, maneuvering between headstones.
As I got closer to the tableau, the pudgy man became my oldest
brother, and, to my amazement, the white-haired old woman my
frail and frightened mother. I stopped for a moment. How small

she looked, how overwhelmed by everything in the world. Where was my father? Then I moved on urgently toward them, suddenly anxious that she see her youngest, lately fifty-five, appear from nowhere.

The Company You (Might) Keep

My publisher recently turned sixty, so, bored with the cliché of whose birthdays one shares, I left him an extended voicemail of the famous who perished at that age. Fascinated by the list, and having recently had a birthday myself, I researched those dead at my own age, potential peeps forever. Morbid? Not at all. Imagine the two of us socially distanced across a table, our cards held close, a kind of Game Macabre for who takes the most tricks. May the best man die.

To wit:

Mark opens with an aggressive throw of Teddy Roosevelt and Leon Trotsky to catch me off guard. I'm left no choice but to counter with Friedrich Nietzsche and Oliver Cromwell. A costly draw. Then he misjudges and drops a weak Calvin Coolidge, tries to bolster the play with Benedict Arnold and Bob Fosse. Forget about it. I come back with Emily Dickinson, Paul Lynde, and, with a dramatic flourish a bigger man would resist, Henry VIII. The latter's a lot to give up early, but it's calculated, a psychological smackdown. My trick, easily. My Jack Ruby and Claude Debussy are no match for Sergio Leone and George Patton. I match his Robert Lowell with Theodore Roethke. Another draw.

Tied. With a smirk, Mark leads with a faux-casual toss of Cyrus the Great, founder of the First Persian Empire, and sweetens the pot with Leonidas I, King of Ancient Sparta. I swallow hard and try a power-play trifecta of Holy Roman Emperors (for which fifty-five was apparently not a fortuitous age)—Frederick II, Charles IV, Henry IV. Not good enough. His Heraclitus is a contested draw with my Lucian. By a hair my Will Rogers edges his Gary Cooper. A heavyweight fight. No quarter given. Still, I'm feeling lucky when I finish out my hand with Gustave Klimt and—sorry, pal—Aesop. Suck on *that* fable! Mark swears and hurls a frowning Henry Gibson. I turn my palms up in commiseration. Welcome to the Big-Boy Table, my friend.

At which point he pauses, and in the horrible seconds that follow I watch a look of bitter resignation transform into that malevolent grin of his. *Gaylord, Gaylord.* He shakes his head sadly at my gullibility, then trumps me with Shemp Howard.

Game over.

Frank Sinatra, Dead on This Day

*[Written May 2020, during self-isolation in Tennessee,
the coronavirus pandemic having canceled our month in
southeast France.]*

May, 1998. We were darting along in our toy rental car, from
Vence just north of the Riviera—where I would be spending the
summer in a cabin writing poems—for an initiating holiday in
the Luberon, stopping overnight in the hilltop village of Mons.
Claudia and I had never been to Provence before. Our first open
market in Grasse that morning, our first *pastis* in an empty café
overlooking the jaw-dropping views surrounding Mons—the
valleys of woodland, the distant slate-blue mountains—that
afternoon. We had already explored the narrow streets, already
entered the *bureau de poste*, mistaking it for the lobby of our
small hotel, and announced to an astonished postmaster "we have
arrived!" That evening, after a nap in the cool, quiet room, we ate
alone in the dining room—Roquefort salad, duck with olives, a
carafe of the proprietor's own red wine. The hotel dog steadfast
and hopeful at our feet.

Early the next day we were on our way. Coffee and pastries at the
bar, the payment of the modest bill, the *Le Figaro* headline. That
buttery Provencal sunlight already hot as we loaded the car. A
slim first volume of my poetry had finally been published. Soon
I'd be up for tenure. It would be another year before we bought
this log house in Tennessee where I currently sit, two before we'd
marry in its yard. That morning in Mons, Claudia so pretty in her
summer dress. We were heading to Bonnieux, a town we'd never
seen, to a B&B where at night one could stand by the pool and
look up at the lit ruins of the Marquis de Sade's castle in Lacoste,
to the season of asparagus and cherries (picked on the whim), to
perfume of rosemary and lavender, to an ideal of a life we fell in
love with if never quite achieved. Not enough time.

But all that was later. At the moment, the Chairman of the Board was dead. I juggled the gearshift, got the toy into first, and off we went.

My Grandmother, Dead at 104

"At 104 she lived through the 1918 pandemic.
Remarkable. These are awful and fragile times."

I'd already returned that morning from picking our first gallon of strawberries of the season, socially distanced in the nearby field that produces each year the sweetest berries we've ever tasted. My wife had returned from the first Friday farmers market, for the first time conducted in masks, with fresh wild salmon and local greens she would later prepare for our dinner, which we would eat on the back deck, by candlelight, in this fine and fleeting May weather.

My father called. The death at 2:00 a.m. My mother currently at the nursing home. She would be a wreck in the days to follow. As a favor to her, I'd tried to contact my grandmother three weeks earlier, on her birthday, when after waiting on hold twice being told by the caretaker, disconcertingly, that "she's sleeping. I tried to wake her but couldn't." The challenge of the funeral in Kentucky, the mess of the safety protocols. Then again, only a handful of family remaining. Restrictions on gatherings not a big problem.

I said goodbye to my wife and drove the convertible out into the country. On a rural lane that slopes and twists past sporadic homes, patches of woods, a few cattle, and a single cantankerous donkey, is a microclimate we've never fathomed, two particular miles of Tennessee backroad the only place outside of Iowa that I've ever seen the red-headed woodpecker, and seen it consistently, two or three on a good day. I walked along in the cool bright afternoon, conspicuous with my binoculars, out in the world after two months of self-isolation, and spotted a bird in minutes: the brilliant red head of its namesake, white breast, black wings with triangular white patches. Gorgeous. Unmistakable. Quick in flight, usually reluctant to being viewed, for the next hour they were everywhere. I hiked all the way to the red barn with its goats and guinea fowl, then back up, between fields of meadow buttercup in bloom, roadsides of large hop clover, ridge of forested hills to the east. Birds flying, birds clinging, birds in and out of two electric pole nesting holes. So many red-headed woodpeckers I quit bothering with the glasses. A dozen. More.

Toward the end, the last rise, the burring of a scarlet tanager, a song I liken to water trickling over stone. A glowing red male in the foliage. The tanager a bird that for many years, for very personal reasons, I have associated with the voices and messages of the dead, and used to rarely hear. The olive-green female is especially shy. One perched in the cedar overhead, calling out above the car. I'm embarrassed to say I think of the female as drab, but this one was lovely, lustrous, watched me with a dark eye not at all tentative. She let me admire and listen for as long as I cared to, remained as I started the engine and pulled away. What did it mean? Probably nothing. What was I feeling? A bit disembodied? Anxious of the future, for my mother and for all of us, yet somehow at peace with everything I couldn't control? Not quite. But it had been a remarkable walk, I was sorry my wife had missed it, and I was anxious to be home with her, sharing the unlikely details.

Desperate for Auguries of Grace

Blue heron in passage as you wait outside the evening's second emergency animal hospital, forbidden to enter due to virus precautions. A cold unseasonal wind you had no time or thought to dress for. Your girl wheeled out of sight—forever?—on the gurney where you lifted her. Shivering at the table outside the hospital, waiting for the telephone jingle, next words, mercy or despair. Whatever was coming, whatever you deserved. You son of a bitch. The way you lived in privilege, appreciated nothing. Fuck you. You *caused* it. The long, slow flapping of the heron against a gray heaven. Signaling.

After the last hour's drive of those stunned, frantic hours, pulling into the dark street of your dark and empty house, a flash of red fox in the headlights, fleeting and ethereal, strong and wild and other, appearing to you, then as quickly returned to its shadow world. Message unclear. No, not unclear. *You. You.*

Yes, get on your knees, you stupid worthless bastard, right there on the porch. Bow your head. Start talking. You fool, you fraud, you hypocrite, ridiculous joke of the universe teaching its lesson. That's right. An angry, powerless, terrified blubbering sham, vowing and bargaining for all the very little you're worth. Yeah. Betraying everything you did or didn't believe, every conviction, without a second thought. Belief doesn't matter. Pride doesn't matter. *Please, please* begged of a moonless night. *Anything you want.* Nothing mattering but the one thing.

Contrition

By midafternoon that Sunday, Lucy was walking unsteadily and there was no longer any pretending something sudden and serious wasn't happening. Without taking time to dress properly, without discussion, we were in the car. I at the wheel, Claudia in the back seat holding her.

By the time they carried our dog out of the first emergency hospital two hours later, and we were driving furiously toward the second, she'd lost all use of her legs. We were given vague and dire prognoses, told that surgery would need to be undertaken immediately if it were to have any chance.

That was Mother's Day. The next nightmarish morning at home, waiting for the phone's percussive signal. "Immediate" revised to within twenty-four hours. The CT scan inconclusive. Further tests. Further waiting. Now afternoon again. An hour passing. What were they *doing*? Then another hour lost. Then at last the diagnosis, the warnings, the costs—yes, yes, please hurry—some estimates of the schedule—*go*, goddamn it, *take care of my girl*—then, finally, horrible math of the clock unstoppable, a time set for the surgery.

The wait for the last call.

I'll keep private the abject details of our fear. But for some unarticulated reason, I stepped into the bathroom, closed the door, looked in the mirror at my red eyes, and began to clip away the beard I'd had since Lucy was a pup small enough to hold in my palm. When I'd pledged to protect her forever. I did the rough work first, scissors pinching at the skin, clumps of white and gray hair falling, then cleaned that away and began, taking my time, with the finishing work—hot water, lather, and razor. Feeling along the jawline for stubble. Meticulous, controlled. Surrendered to my helplessness. When I'd finished, I was looking at a stranger. They were about to cut into her. Fate would have its way with us.

When we picked up Lucy for four days later, she came out walking. A large patch on her back, her front legs, chest, and wrinkled throat shaved clean of that beautiful white coat. Looking so small and fragile, but walking. I think I understood then what I had tried to do. However irrational, however foolish. We were in this together. Whatever rough shape we might be in at the moment, and whatever would come next. I lifted her into the back seat, into Claudia's arms.

With Virus Deaths in the US to Surpass 100,000 by Memorial Day, Nature Continues in Her Season

The fledging cardinal on the gravel drive unambiguous in its hungry squawk to harried father. Our blueberry bushes heavy with darkening fruit. Chickadees have quickly nested the evacuated bluebird box. A clutch of five white eggs smaller than jelly beans, speckled red, although the mother loudly disapproves of my visit and cares nothing for my good intentions.

A rumor that our resident turkey hen, Mary Jane, has seven chicks, a formidable responsibility. She was seen earlier today, so I am told, ushering them out of sight into the bloomed-out scapes of the iris bed. The same bed from which a single baby rabbit, tiny thing, has boldly emerged to nibble on an edge of lawn effusive with clover.

And yes, the neighbor's black cat, admittedly beautiful in her own right, stealthily along the fence row. Such is the manner of the world. I have shooed her away. For the moment.

Golden Retriever

Après surgery, Lucy must now wear a harness, and I am checking out at the pet superstore with a design that looks comfortable, in pink, when a golden retriever bounds in with her owner. A beautiful, healthy mutt, with a full and lustrous coat, crazy-goofy smile, and energy to spare. As they approach the door of the grooming station, she is exultant, no place she'd rather be and straining toward what's next. I notice, though, that she walks with an odd, sweeping motion, bowing a bit in each stride and using a lot of space. When I look closer, I see her right front paw is missing. And I wince.

Over the years, I've crossed paths with a few three-legged dogs. I remember each encounter vividly. In part, I think, due to their uniform exuberance, their absolute joy and absorption in the immediate moment and its opportunity for scandal, hobbling along without blame or complaint or even courage. They're simply ready to roll! These dogs would be mystified by my pity, and this shames me. The missing paw is somehow, perhaps, even worse. So close to a perfectly complete creature, so heartbreakingly far. And yet. A short-haired terrier enters, and the retriever gambols awkwardly toward it, an expansive, dipping shuffle. She is all over the new arrival—wagging, sniffing, tongue lolling, not knowing or caring what the hell I'm musing about as I recite my customer ID to the cashier.

That was more than a week ago, and I've thought of that damned dog, too dumb with happiness to know how miserably afflicted she is, every day since. Days during which Lucy, in her snazzy new harness, endures the daily therapy on each leg—massaging the muscles, then sets of bending at the joints—necessary for her best recovery.

Korean Air Flight #008

Some may still recall that on Thursday, September 1, 1983, KAL-008 deviated into prohibited airspace and was shot down by a Soviet Su-15 interceptor, crashing the Boeing 747 into the Sea of Japan and killing all 269 passengers and crew on board. I do. I had been on that same flight number seven days earlier, returning from Seoul to New York, refueling in Anchorage. I was eighteen, excited to be coming home from a summer in Asia, including several weeks in China before it had widely opened to Westerners, a trip I was too callow to truly appreciate. I have the regrettable photos and lovesick journal to prove the latter, if proof be required. A boy coming home with tales to tell and exotic secrets to withhold, bleary and emotional from the dark, twenty-hour flight.

In succeeding years, accruing now to four decades, I've periodically considered the tragedy of that downed plane. Not profoundly, not proprietarily or with any sense of epiphany, rather in a random, perusing sort of way. The inescapable "What If?" My parents would have suffered the worst and most immediately, of course. Otherwise, what difference? Intersections with other lives never missed because they never happened, another mute shape amid the great jumble of ghosts, tenebrous, grotesque with envy, that crowd the earth, perhaps a hand passing unnoticed near the face of a dear woman not my wife, a beloved dog devoted to another, the friends and rivals of other men.

And so on. I had a life I was anxious to live, and I was extended the opportunity to live it, and an abstraction of 269 deaths—pointless? edifying?—by which to consider its failures, its modest and fleeting glories, its countless aircraft rising out of my control into the dangerous sky. A blinding explosion of fire, a scream of rent steel. Nothing.

June Returns

And brings its inquisitional heat, blurring thought and judgment. I don't know if the oncoming pickup's cough of horn signals expletive or approval, but the truck slows as I rush for the turtle, wide as a dinner plate, paused in the lane. This is not the first snapper I've ever grabbed by its bony shell, but, even as the blunt black beak snaps backward, there's no time to hesitate. A foul ooze of mud all over my hands, clawed toes squirming, tail whipping. I lift it and jog out of the road. Dizzy fragments. My convertible, idling illegally in the intersection, unnerved wife as passenger, edge of desiccated field being razed and paved by the Baptist church, no good place to release the monster as it snaps its head toward me, furious to take a finger to teach me the lesson of my good intentions. I keep moving, gazing into the pink maw, at the fat wet tongue fluttering, into the blind wound of a missing eye, then free the cursed thing a few feet into parched weeds, raise my stinking hands, and dodge to the car.

Without speaking, my wife tears me an antibacterial wipe from the roll, then another, and a third as I drop a gloppy mess onto the floorboard. I feel lightheaded, breathless, engine rumbling in park, vehicles pausing and passing at the stop, thin screen between sanity and panic. We drive on, arrive at last at the city square, first Saturday farmers market of the season, straight into a knot of traffic. Bodies crowd and surge between tables, disdainful of placards exhorting a safe distance. Not one face mask in sight. May was a third month of loss and chronic illness, of isolation, and June has begun the same. What will the next days and weeks bring? How will we live? When my wife looks out over the snarl of our town, the community we've mingled happily among for many years, early summer produce, she sees nothing but death. There is no way in hell, or in god's name, I will coax her to step among them.

Doolittle

"Gay-*lord*, you ever meet Old Man Flem? Ran the paper mill till it burned?"

"Uh, hm. I don't, uh . . ."

"But you must'a known his grandson, Tater? Used to steal copper wiring and try to sell it out the back of that rusted-out van of his?"

"Mmmm . . ."

"Tater never was too sharp a pencil. I 'member one summer, never forget, Tater and Jimmy Horn's boy, Jimmy Jr.?, was in here with a load of somebody's two-by-fours . . ."

At which point Doolittle's thick hands rest on my shoulders, the red face beneath his white crewcut creases into a smile, his shoulders begin shaking in a genuine, honest-to-god, old-school chuckle, and the tale resumes.

When Doolittle sold his namesake barber shop and retired, he got zoned for a single chair in his double-wide, in an independent room busy with news clippings, photos, annotated menus, cartoons of Hillary Clinton, a case of vintage straight razors, combs, and tonics for sale. Good luck for me, as he's a neighbor, and for years I've had only to walk down my street, cross the two lanes of Highway 96, and angle through his yard to enter a remnant of how it was. Doolittle's is a community crossroads, and I've nodded in introduction to many atavistic characters while I was draped in the chair getting a close cut. Coffee drunk, legends revisited, opinions confirmed, current work ethics criticized, culinary fare fondly invoked. Politics never arise, however, not explicitly, a concession I believe to my presence—a seemingly nice-enough young fellow but only recently moved here twenty years ago and also rumored to teach at the "university." Best tread softly.

Doolittle is a compendium of local lore: He knows who did it, who failed to do it, who got caught trying to do it, whom he was related to, when, where, and why it happened, and what went wrong. Those controlling hands setting the pace, the intimacy of the blades. Trimmed ears and eyebrows, flourish of warm towel to massage the neck signaling that your turn is over. The spinning of the chair for approval in the mirror. A roll of cash fished out of his pocket thick enough to choke a horse.

Once, I walked home with a three-pound roll of hot pork sausage made by the blah-blah brothers down the road in Milton. Doolittle happened to have an extra log in his fridge and insisted I try it. The sausage was excellent.

All that abruptly halted with COVID-19. For me, anyway. For all I know, Doolittle has plied his trade throughout these stressful months, held court without interruption, and, I'm certain, without mask or distancing or other Democrat silliness. Last week, as I knelt bare-chested on the porch, attacking my mop of hair with a handheld mirror and a newly purchased "home haircutting system," slowly building nerve for the shorter attachments, practicing blending of top and sides, tapering the ears, absolutely butchering my neckline, eyes blurry with sweat as I tried to decipher the brochure tips through steamed glasses, it occurred to me I wouldn't be returning to the chair across the street. Doolittle will never read this and it's unlikely we'll see each other again—maybe a wave sometime. (He's an admirer of my Thunderbird.) The quarter mile between our houses the distance between two worlds. The cut looked passable. Good enough. Better next time. Everything ends, often suddenly and without announcement, a lesson that this year seems to be teaching determinedly. And just as I've long suspected.

End of Season: Local Strawberries

After the night's persistent patter of rain, the field shouldn't be open this morning. But the sun's out and I have a premonition. Sure enough, although the crowd of weeks ago is absent, the gates are open. I ask the old man if the season's over, and he confirms that, yep, today's likely the last. I translate his slurry of accent: "If it's red, ya better pick it."

Good advice. And yes, weedy plants and muddy trenches announce the end. Many of the berries, turned over in the hand, show bruise and wound, reminding me of the gruesome finale of a pink salmon run I witnessed in Alaska. The plants have done their work of procreation.

It requires the patient culling of two rows, sweaty labor in the late May sun, but I collect a gorgeous gallon of berries: glowing, firm, sweet. Perfection in a world too often blind to it. These have ruined us for the sour, monstrous impostors sold for nothing at the grocer. When we moved to Lascassas (pop. 120) two decades ago, the strawberry field (owned by Pearcy, who also of course owns the Mercantile) was an unexpected boon. The best strawberries we'd ever tasted (rivaled only by a midsummer yield I discovered in Costa Rica, in the region around Poás Volcano), and an annual pleasure we anticipate. I often travel during much or all of May, so, plans canceled due to pandemic, the ripening arrived as welcome distraction in a month of isolation, worry, family illness, family death.

The most enjoyed berries, arguably, are those eaten as they're plucked from the vine, a warm and illicit buffet. But who can argue with a freshly washed bowl, each berry lifted by its leafy stem, casually consumed as one reads? Or dipped into a ramekin of sweetened condensed milk (a trick from Costa Rica, *vide supra*) or powdered sugar? I baked repeated batches of savory shortcake biscuits, with rosemary from the garden and just a touch of sweetness. Split one, smother it with chopped berries macerated for a few hours in sugar or, if one's feeling tony, balsamic vinegar and tarragon, top with whipped cream and imagine all that's lost will be restored. A strawberry buttermilk cake, with crunchy topping of turbinado sugar burned into the crust. Strawberry-honey ice cream and a twist of cracked black pepper. A strawberry crisp loaded with butter (I may have lied about the amount), its rich and textured topping of oats, brown sugar, cinnamon. We finished it and I made another. Panic baking? I had time on my hands, while distraction and pleasure remained in short supply.

My wife and I easily, unapologetically ate five gallons this month and wish the season weren't over, a sweet taste of our life as we remember it and have come to expect it. I nod to the old man—when Pearcy's wife's not on the prowl, there's no extra charge for topping off your bucket—shout that I'll see him next year, and head for the car. Next year. Not something to have ever taken for granted.

End of Season: Louisiana Crawdads

The cold, sucked-out heads from ten pounds of crawdad constitute a fine if dizzying breakfast, fit for a king—Creole, Cajun, otherwise. Twist abdomen from carapace and claws, scissor through the shell, pop the tail flesh loose, suck the spicy goodness from the head, discard. A fluid, economical rhythm you settle into, a three-bowl affair: medium bowl for fistfuls of chilled bodies lifted from the stock pot for easy access, large for shells and heads, small for the plump pink tails. Woozy and entranced from the unctuous brains and goop, fingers burning from the cayenne, you find your pace, keep cracking, keep sucking.

With our local seafood store forced closed by the pandemic, I nearly missed crawdad season altogether and had to face the real and horrible possibility of no parcels of crawdad dressing in the freezer to get me through the hard months surely to follow, their moments of primordial trial and existential drought. It was a tense time.

Then I heard the rumor, followed the gossip, and sure enough Bubba was back in business for pick-up. I did my research. *Call Thursday afternoon. No guarantees.* At last, the day came. At 2:00 p.m. I made the call. The truck had arrived! Within forty minutes, a squirming sack of big, beautiful, crimson mudbugs was on ice in my trunk as I hurried home to boil them up, heavy on the seasoning. The power of prayer.

Re the dressing: For measures of ingredients, trust your judgment according to experience, instinct, and verve. I assume that after you boiled your crawdads the evening before (for the next morning's extraction), you then made your skillet of cornbread. As you will, simply crumble the bread into your largest mixing bowl, add plenty of onion sautéed in butter, grated sharp cheddar, diced jalapeños (be bold, friend), chicken stock, salt, black pepper, and a farm egg, finally and with love folding in the whole tails. Into a greased baking dish, a hot oven for forty-five minutes. Brown the top under the broiler.

The biggest challenge is not to eat so many tails during the night, as tonic to fearful dream or paean to good fortune, however you're personally disposed, that by dawn you've sabotaged the project and must begin anew. "Our wills and fates do so contrary run . . ." If it happens, it happens. Forgive yourself as ye would forgive the world, say your prayers again, make a call.

Path of Totality

Our little town nearly abutted the southern boundary of the projected pathway, a diagonal belt across the country, but there we were, somewhere between Cape Girardeau and Greenville, fully within the totality. I had returned from Alaska a week early, had equipped us with dubious eyewear from China but also a pair of higher-end "EclipSmart" Celestron magnifying viewers with guaranteed "solar safe filter technology." You bet.

We'd moved the Adirondack chairs into the yard, into the blazing midday August heat. The show began at noon precisely, central time, and we circled from house to chairs, increasingly anxious, giddy beneath the graying sky. The science promised us, between ninety-minute windows of waning and waxing, one minute and eight seconds.

As the central moment loomed, we took our seats in the theater of lawn and darkened woods, anchored to the earth, replenished mimosas in hand, hearts loud.

When it came, it came fast. The sun disappeared. The temperature plummeted. All birds went silent. Mars appeared, Venus. Mosquitoes. Lightning bugs. It was, in short, the damnedest physical phenomenon I've ever experienced. Instant transport to a different world, out of sync of reason or belief. A world where day was night, where one might look directly, unharmed, at the burning ring of the sun. I exhorted my wife to remove her glasses. The minute passing. *Now*, I shouted, and she joined me in gazing, in its glorious seconds, at this fleeting apocalypse.

Caution Fatigue

I'd not seen my father for five months, and, during that time, my mother only for a few moments at a cemetery. An unprecedented length of time. Somewhere in those dates of "sheltering in place," my dad's eighty-eighth birthday, my own birthday, Momo's death, another Mother's Day come and gone. The world didn't promise to be safer any time soon, so I loaded the car with two coolers of food and drink, a few gifts and surprises, face masks, antiviral wipes, all the absurd rules I'd outlined in advance for the visit. No kisses, no hugs, as much distance as the small rooms allowed. Well, we'd see how that went.

The drive north uneventful—backroads, state border crossing, sunny afternoon, loud rude music for distraction, all well until I turned onto Anchor Avenue and saw the house, the bushy lawn, the garden, the recent spruce stump, the flagpole. I pulled into the drive and sat idling. They would never visit us again, waving and honking as the Buick pulled away until next time. And any visit of mine now could be the last. The latter always the case, of course, but the math had become suffocating. All those weekends and holidays, fun meals and stories, schemes, derisive laughs. The years. I sat waiting, listening to the growl of the engine, indulging. Then tamping it down, composing my ridiculous self. A robin returned to her nest in a spindly crabapple. It was a sweltering day.

Come on. Pull it together. Like the man said: Smile.

I got out of the car, punched in the security code—their wedding date of sixty-seven years ago. The door rose. Then I drove into the shadows of the garage, took a breath, and, like the lucky bastard that I've always been, went in to greet my sad, beautiful parents.

Three Meals of Memory

Goat Brain Curry: Old Delhi, Dec. 2007

Sunil, director of the Global Arts Village, navigated us through the clamor and aromatic chaos at a periphery of the markets to a plain open restaurant of plastic tables and chairs. Weeks later, I was still thinking about the unctuous yellow plate, scooped up in torn naan delivered hot from the adjacent ovens. The richest dish I've ever eaten, a dizzying taboo. I hailed a rickshaw outside the suburb of Ghitorni, back into the old city. To hell with poetry that day. Through chutzpah and luck, and patience with wrong turns, I found the restaurant, and the curry, again.

Camel Tongue Sandwich: Fez, May 2019

I'd abandoned the others, assured them of my instincts for direction, and plunged into the chaos of Fez-al-Bali. The hellish tanneries, men hip-deep and bent to its vats of blood-red dye, the stretched hides, the touristic sprig of mint offered to cover the stench, had made an impression. I needed to get lost, some manageable trouble.

The battered copper pots steamed with tongues of all sizes. I gestured toward a huge and bobbing camel option. The big, blank-faced fellow wrestled the appendage onto a board, attacked it with a blade, and stuffed the grilled *batbout*. Assessing me, he raised his thick brow, gestured toward his back and shoulders. When I didn't understand, he repeated the gesture. *Ah!* Yes, please, and a bonus whack of camel hump tucked in with the rest. I sat across the alleyway on a stool, the soft, chewy bread bulging with slices of tender tongue, hump boiled to gelatinous perfection.

One year before the world contracted.

Death Row Last Meal: Nashville, Feb. 19, 2020

Nicholas Sutton, executed the following evening by electric chair and pronounced dead at 7:26 p.m., CT.

Both the *Tennessean* and local NPR affiliate felt compelled to report, without explanation, the details of his final request. Months later, all these weeks and days and moments of self-isolation, for some reason I still recall the menu: fried pork chops, mashed potatoes and gravy, peach pie with vanilla ice cream. I can't seem to forget.

Last Words for Now

Summer solstice. The circle nearly complete of my year of witnessing, of simply paying attention. A new moon, so the night to follow this longest day, nearing its end, will be a dark one. But darkness comforts, and I welcome it. I sit on a stepping stone, legs in the cool grass, stroking Lucy's fur as she lies beside me. The shaved spot from her surgery scruffy with new growth. I rub for luck. She's still with me. She too likes the quiet, the arrival of night. When I was a child, the humid June air glowed with lightning bugs. In later years, they disappeared completely. Now, a few have returned. Who can foresee the migration of what will come, the final cost of what we bought or sold? Across these reckless Southern states, infections and deaths have spiked again, as easily prophesied. I watch one insect's blink of light, try to anticipate where in the dimming sky it will next announce itself. Beneath my open hand, Lucy's back rises and lowers in breath, my sweet old dog looking out over whatever it is that she beholds. Don't let anyone tell you I didn't love the world, cherish my little bit of time. I wish we could stay here together forever, just like this.

Returning

Out of a million moments, mostly lost, a fragment preoccupies me. It is late afternoon, sun noticeably in descent, and I am alone on a train returning from a day's excursion. I've no recollection what that self-styled adventure might have been, the allure of its distraction, what country I am in, nor whether it is ten years ago or perhaps twenty. But this younger man is pleasantly tired, lulled by the click of the wheels, sipping a discreet drink, and, the seats beside and across from him empty, paid ticket in pocket, reclining comfortably in his good fortune. With the train's on-time departure, he feels a successful day officially concluded. The remnants of the city left behind, fields pass in red and gold striations of light, a movie unreeling for his sole benefit. The geometry of tillage, the strutting inspections of ravens, perhaps a surveying glide of raptor, or even, if it's a truly lucky day, and it has been, a red fox emerged from adjacent woods, glimpsed only for seconds. Across the world are those he loves and misses with a bittersweet longing. He is likely returning to a gathering of writers or artists, returning later than his usual routine, and this breaking of habit, a modest and private violation, is itself pleasurable. Likely, there will be just time for a quick shower and change into clean pants and shirt before his tardy arrival to dinner, the tale of the day anxious for the telling. But for now, unwashed, soothed in the cool cabin of his passage, sun ever lower, this fair landscape never to be seen again, all suspended in a fine amber. A friend recently wrote me, *I have forgotten so much of my life*. Why does this moment return now, vivid and haunting?

Poetry in the Vines

Later that afternoon, we would visit the grave of Cesare Pavese in the *cimetero* of Santo Stefano Belbo, and after our respects and photo ops, on the shaded terrace of a bar off the *piazza*, toast the poet with a glass of the local moscato—a light translucent gold in color, aromas of citrus, cold and delicately bubbling. (My third collection of poems, *Four Nails*, took its title—as well as its section epigraphs—from Pavese's remarkable diaries. "One nail drives out another. But four nails make a cross.")

We felt we'd earned the drink. I'd skimmed some suspect literature, and that morning we'd embarked on a leap of faith. But yes, the Piemonte hilltop village of Castiglione Tinella, its views and thousand-year history, await discovery by any fool of fortune. If you've no better sense than to start out on foot "from the central square, pass behind the school building, on road 51 south . . . but after twenty meters turn right on a slope between houses, near the old walnut tree" and onward, you will find yourself among the sloping vines, hilltop farmhouses above, receding ridges of oak and hazelnut and poplar, valleys opening, puzzled workers at lunch watching as you go. And yes, in the distance, between terraced rows, a poem declaiming itself to the sky! And you are far from America, from Hollywoodland.

Six poems are spread among these hills of grapes, available by various hiking paths. Trusting the red and yellow wooden arrows will lead you past two of the displayed verses, both by Lorenzo Dulevant and of a theme. "*Verrà scalza / come faceva nei balli dell'estate . . .*" The lines, their white letters perhaps six feet in height, approach and recede, twist and obscure as one climbs, dips, slides. After one gambols with tone, nuance of image, caress of metaphor, and has mangled the phrases beyond recognition, a posted barcode and one's wife's iPhone offer rescue: "She will come barefoot / as in the summer dances / giving me Moscato grapes / sweet as her eyes / as sweet as her blood." Pretty good, and why not!? Hell, you're in Italy, aren't you? Sun sultry overhead, vines writhing, fruit ripening, hills and valleys undulating . . . ?

After all, not every day does one stumble through the "country of the written vines." A place, a culture, and a people to actually enact and maintain such a misty-eyed concept? Sigh. We trudged along, crossed a country road, circled back toward the north side of Castiglione Tinella and its "imposing parish church," climbed a hot dusty trail to reach the "beautiful laurel tree" and vantage over the valleys' "arena of vineyards," not another tourist and/or poet in sight.

As we completed the loop and were reentering the village along a row of young olive trees, a second poem appeared, angling away on the nearest hill: *"Fermati/qui è passato un carro con le uve/nel silenzio più alto . . ."* I rolled the words over my thirsty tongue, tasting the possibilities of my poor but spirited Italian, then cut Signor Dulevant a break and ceded to technology: "Stop right there / a cart with grapes has passed / in veiled silence / a man has passed / with all his suffering."

Hassan II Mosque, Casablanca

. . . the throne of Allah was built on water
—Qur'an

Lazing bare-footed on the cool carpet, sandals in a plastic sack beside me, how clever I was. Having roamed the dusty streets for hours, first full day in the city, I turned tired and parched and without thinking as the 1:00 p.m. call to prayer began, started across a cracked field toward the beckoning green tiles of the minaret, the great mosque hulking over the sea. As I approached, a rough plan formed. *Look stern. Keep your mouth shut.* A boy at the entrance stopped me and barked a challenge. Someone barked at him in return. As he appraised me further, I scowled and shrugged, kept moving.

Hundreds of men gradually entered. An astonishingly beautiful space capable of holding 25,000, the two-hundred-foot high domed ceiling glistening, the warm marble archways, the ornate pulpit. I stretched out my legs and soaked it all in. As the *iman* began the first prayer, I remained quiet and respectful. *Salah*, second pillar of Islam. Piece of cake. It wasn't until the men, now numbering a thousand or more, rose and crowded in unison the western end of the hall, reassembled as a tight single entity facing Mecca, that I realized the extent of my arrogance, felt an unfolding and palpable danger. I knew I couldn't risk approach, could not join them and mimic the rising prayer. The group bent to its knees. The verses grew louder.

I was afraid. Physically afraid as I couldn't recall ever being. Interloper, infidel, idiot, entirely of my own doing. As I stood rigid against an arched column, I cannot begin to convey my conspicuousness. I was alone, exposed, breathing hard. A guard watched me. Vaguely, I parroted the collective gestures. If it came to it, I could bolt across the enormous floor, but even if I succeeded in reaching those closed bronze doors?

What could I do, now that I had maneuvered myself into this place and instant of my life? The chanting continued—faithful, emphatic. I understood nothing, had no notion of what might come next. What would happen, would happen. I had sought it out. In the minutes that followed, that seemed to stretch into eternity, with no better idea for salvation, I got on my knees, bowed my head, closed my eyes, and surrendered to whatever power would decide my fate.

Closing Thoughts for Chauncey Gardiner

It's a good garden and a healthy one; its trees are healthy and so are its shrubs and flowers, as long as they are trimmed and watered in the right season. The garden needs a lot of care. I do agree with the President: everything in it will grow strong in due course. And there is still plenty of room in it for new trees and new flowers of all kinds.

— Jerzy Kosiński

Ah, Chance, my dear friend; ah, the President; ah, how the garden has altered. Perennials struggle to survive the torrid temperatures or simply succumb. Annuals from years past rise and flourish. Nature is upended. The garden doesn't want apologies. Hydrangeas covet the shade yet require continual watering. Why one branch blooms its ball of blue, another of pink, another not at all, remains an answer to the question one struggles to ask. Dragon wing begonias react poorly to overwatering, waxy leaves pale and defeated. Vinca major, cut to the ground, rebounds undeterred. The Japanese painted ferns, the small dark jungle of Mexican petunia, shivering beneath respective showers, live together without boundaries. Zinnias promote their shameless color, hibiscus bow beneath heavy buds of a show soon to commence. But spiderwort is finished. The clematis grown from seed, clinging weakly to the trellis, has yellowed and perished. These are the lessons of the garden. It needs more care than ever. It cannot sustain itself. And to where may the caretaker turn? To plant and organize the map of the garden. To serve with patience and resolve. To water, weed, and prune. To be ridiculed. Even to be banished. Ah, Chance, the cruel changes rung.

Yes, granted, daylilies in full season. Today, one hundred and eight blooms of twenty-six varieties. An impressive bouquet. They grow healthy and strong. I pray a storm will not destroy them. Each June morning begins with deadheading, tender and brutal work so that new flowers may display without distraction of what came before. Each to its private schedule, to its breeding and the reverence of the gardener. Goodbye this morning to Dance Ballerina Dance, so brief. Welcome to As We Were and the single scape it offers. Here is the water. Here is the sun.

CODA

pre-pandemic

Dyea, Alaska, Doesn't Even Exist

One gambler who came up before Steele was contemptuous when the policeman fined him fifty dollars.

"Fifty dollars—is that all? I've got that in my vest pocket,"
he said.

Whereupon the Superintendent added: ". . . and sixty days on the woodpile. Have you got that in your vest pocket?"
—Pierre Berton, *The Klondike Fever*

Here's a photograph: I am standing at the edge of the Nelson Slough at high tide, the water curving out of the frame as it snakes through the Dyea Flats. In both hands, I grip a pink salmon caught moments ago, the distinctive hump identifying a male, the long thin jowl open as if striking the air. Rising in the distance behind us, the snow-capped mountains that ring the inlet. In my borrowed rubber boots and feigned expression of solemn respect for this ugly fish I've just bludgeoned with the handle of my net, I try to look the part. And sound the part, too. The fellow who took the photo asks me how to clean his own pink. "Underneath, cut it from the head down," I say.

I'm not a fisherman, but the pinks are starting to run, I'm in Alaska, I've read too many books for my own good, and it all gets under my skin. No need to charter a boat—for the first time in memory, kings are mandatory throw-back due to low numbers, so I'd only be going out after pinks, anyway. The slough is only four miles from the cabin, straight down the Dyea (pronounced *dye-EE*) Road on my bicycle, then, just before the Taiya River Bridge, a right turn toward the Dyea Townsite and the flats. So I hitch a ride into Skagway, buy a three-day fishing license I don't need, two hooks that I do, grab a copy of *Dot's Fishing Guide 2017 Tide Tables*, and I'm ready for some theater.

The pinks are mostly male, crazed with rutting, and in no mood to eat. The fish in the photo I hooked in the side just by dragging a barb through the water. The next day, I hook another male, deep in the dorsal fin. This method is neither skilled nor remotely mythical, but both fish put up a good, muscular fight. They're in no mood to eat or to die, either. They're in the mood to rut. I clean the bodies on the bank of the West Creek, fifty yards from my cabin, tossing heads, fins, and guts out into the current and splashing blood stains with the silty water so as not to encourage bears.

I fillet the flesh, fighting the pin bones, make a barbeque sauce of ketchup, garlic, Tabasco, and a jar of dark molasses I oddly inherited in the empty pantry, and light the grill. I've been told by actual fisherman that the offal is inedible, or that anyway it had occurred to no one to try to eat it. I brown a liver in butter in a skillet on the gas stove, and a heart, and something long and pure white I believe to be a swim bladder, and eat them. The possible bladder is especially delicious, a soft and creamy texture. Two days of blood and killing are sufficient to satisfy the fishing urge. I'm part pink salmon now.

⁊❧

During my six weeks in Dyea, I bicycle to the flats two to three times each week. Four miles, through the last of summer's wild irises, over the Nelson Slough Bridge, and there I am. Drop the bike in an inconspicuous spot in the undergrowth and start walking south. Not once do I fail to see bald eagles, both adults and juveniles in the spruce thick on the eastern mountain face. Perched, flying north or south, cartwheeling on at least one occasion. I am often the only human out near the shoreline, navigating the mud and sand, the puddles and sea grasses. Curiously, out here is the only spot in the entire Dyea area where I am able to get a cell phone signal, albeit a spotty one when it's windy. And there's no public phone anywhere, of course. So I make my periodic calls home sitting on a favorite fallen tree, now driftwood long burnished by water and sun to a smooth shade of bone. Low tide exposes the wooden posts of the old town's wharf of more than a century ago, rows of black and rotted teeth jutting in lines from the sand. Further out at the water's edge, always the silhouette of three or four blue herons. Once, the tide forcing me to move north, I see a harbor seal's slick, bald head pop up in the rising slough. Brown bears, I'm told, come down in the summer in the evening to fish. (By the time of those late northern twilights, I am at the cabin well into my cups. Biking to the flats to surprise a ten-foot, thousand-pound carnivore at dinner seems ill-advised.)

Harbor seals are common in the Taiya River, which runs along the western border of the flats. One day I "borrow"—I didn't technically ask my host—a car, the windshield-cracked, mud-caked model preferred here, and drive the stunning nine-mile curving route from Dyea to Skagway on the newly widened and smoothed Dyea Road. It's the only road to and through Dyea, and the stretch west and above the flats is carved out of the mountain and follows the river. Starting out for Skagway in the morning, I stop to photograph two mature bald eagles on a log during low tide, just below me on the flats. Curving back that afternoon—to return the Toyota before it's discovered missing, I hope—I stop again, now high tide. The river is full of seals. One, two, three, a half dozen. Who knows how many? Heads rise, vanish.

The flats are always breathtaking, whether on chilly, atmospheric days with the mountains lost in cloud, or when the cover breaks, the sun returns, and sky and distances open up. The binoculars, the camera, they do nothing justice. After the first visits, I quit taking pictures and focus instead on the moment. Standing out there, I am at the edge of something special, a small part of a thing vast, and, hell yes, holy. Only a visitor, I nevertheless feel I deserve to be there and am welcome.

❧

Mostly, my company at the homestead is non-human, and there's plenty of it. Officially: two horses (Glory and Twilight), a pair of miniature pigs (her name I forget; the smaller male is Boarus—get it?), two ducks, one beehive, one noisy and clock-challenged rooster and his harem of twenty black-and-white striped Plymouth Rock chickens from whom I regularly steal a streaked egg or two, cradled clandestinely, carefully in the pockets of my denim jacket for the trek back to the cabin. I throw the chickens a handful of cracked corn now and then. We call it even.

Oh, and the dogs. The dogs. They are easily an exposé unto themselves. Mya, the golden retriever always ready to romp, ideally in the form of chasing sticks—with which she never returns—in the West Creek, then loping back up to the drive dripping wet for a good roll in the dirt. If I am sitting on the front porch reading, it's not uncommon for Mya to bring a stone to be thrown and drop it at my feet. If I manage to angle it into the weeds, I buy enough time to read a paragraph. A short one. Taiya, the gorgeous German shepherd who is sometimes social, sometimes thoughtful and withdrawn, quietly runs the pack. She's good company on a walk for anyone nervous of bears. And then there's Hudson. I don't know what the hell Hudson is—some kind of hound, I suppose. What he really is, is goofy and rough. If something's on your lap or the rickety side table, good luck—it's likely about to go flying. Here's Hudson, ready to go! Hold on.

My favorite visitations, though, are the wild and unexpected ones. The deer mouse, lightning fast and cute as a button with its bug eyes, that I feed peanuts and sunflower seeds on the porch in the days' last light. The small inquisitive red squirrels and aggressive Steller's jays. The even more raucous raven pair gliding through the shadows of the big cottonwoods. My favorite of all, when I open the window above the kitchen sink, and, turning away, hear a thud—a brown bat rudely awakened and dislodged, sprawled on the sill, and as surprised as I, one leathery wing draped on either side. Its tufted ears, attentive yellow gaze, low sustained hiss from between tiny rows of teeth. I let the bat make up its own mind about our next move, and after a few minutes of recovery it chooses to fly out, not in. Just as well. I imagine it an angelic visit and torture that odd conceit in a poem. The dead vole—long story—I bury in the sandy soil beneath a purple hyssop blossom, the grave within view of my writing table.

᠔

A month in, I do finally see my bear. I've taken the narrow-rail train up over the dizzying White Pass (from sea level at Skagway to 2,865 feet at the summit) and into the Yukon, to the town of Carcross, as far as the line now goes. On the ride back down the Klondike Highway, we see a small black bear, cinnamon-colored and handsome by the side of the road, an odd place for it this time of year now that the dandelions, a favorite snack, have bloomed out. The bear seems unimpressed, giving us plenty of time to hang out of windows for blurry photographs and movies. It squats, defecates. The van is abuzz, laughing. We're all thrilled. Then it ambles back into the woods, its mother around somewhere.

᠔

> "There ain't no choice," said an old-timer of choosing between the Chilkoot and the White Pass. "One's hell. The other's damnation."
> —Martha Ferguson McKeown

The Dyea Townsite gets described as a ghost town, but walking the grid of pathways under a canopy of spruce, hemlock, cottonwood, and lodgepole pine, I don't see any apparitions. I don't see much of anything. A single propped-up facade of a building. A depression in the ground that could have been an outhouse or a cellar. Out to the east, a sweep of meadow dotted with summer wildflowers. The fact is, Dyea no longer exists, ghostly or otherwise.

This was Gold Rush country, though there was never gold here. In the Inner Passage, Skagway and Dyea were overwhelmed with stampeders, each posed beside his one ton of goods—a year's worth of supplies—mandated for each man by the Canadian government (it's a fascinating list—10 lbs. coffee, 15 lbs. salt, *150 lbs.* bacon!, one can mustard . . .). The blurry photos of the crowded Dyea wharf, compared to the solitude of the flats today, astound, are hard to fathom. From Skagway, stampeders took the White Pass into Canada and the Yukon. From Dyea, the Chilkoot Trail. The White Pass was nicknamed the Dead Horse Trail after the three thousand abused and overloaded pack animals were left dead there in 1898. The shorter Chilkoot Trail features a thousand-foot climb named (cynically?) the Golden Stairs, climbed single-file. At one point, the trail rises nearly 2,500 feet in three and a half miles. (Jack London took the Chilkoot in late 1897. I hiked the trail's "easy" beginning one sunny afternoon—to Finnegan's Point and the ethereal Irene's Glacier—carrying no pack, and ten miles in and out, four hard hours, was every bit of fun I needed.) By 1897, after only a few months, Dyea was a boomtown of an estimated eight thousand, with 150 businesses (hotels, restaurants, saloons, outfitters). By 1903—the dream of gold already long dead and the completion of a White Pass railroad from Skagway having put the final nail into Dyea's coffin—the population is reported to have been . . . three. As weeks pass, I hear stories and legends endlessly. Happy endings are hard to come by.

There's nothing here now but the trees and some recently repaved paths (everyone I talk with liked it better before the repaving). Houses were moved or sold as lumber or burned or flooded by a shifting Taiya River. There was a lot more water here 120 years ago. The whole area of the flats is undergoing a geological process called "glacial rebound," the land rising at an astounding rate of .75 inches per year, which translates into a valley floor more than eight feet higher than it was a century ago, when flooding in the town would have been common. So, the con men and prostitutes and broken and exploited miners, the whole rapacious dream, all long departed. A couple of miles north the Dyea Road passes here.

A handful of eccentric homesteaders, mostly hidden, live off the road. The year-rounders. The serious freaks. But here in town this afternoon it's just me and the young forest. A single grouse, the darting shape of a field mouse or vole, a score of glaucous-wing gulls circling the river. The golden sky.

ॐ

> For some goldseekers, Slide Cemetery was only one of
> several burials.
>
> —on-site placard

But if it's ghosts we crave, it's ghosts we'll have. They're not hard to rouse. Leaving the flats and townsite, turn left at the Slide Cemetery Road for a community of a different sort, one with a personally disconcerting twist. Another photograph, then many more, of thin wooden markers, leaning and decayed, facsimiles of markers rotted away before them. James Edward Doran, Age twenty-one, Native Minnesota, Died April 3, 1898, RIP. S. Grimes, Tacoma, Wash., Died April 3, 1898. John A Morgan, Emporia, Kansas, Died April 3, 1898. S. Atkins, Barker City, Oregon, Died, April 3, 1898. The names, the cities from which the men arrived, and that single date again and again as I browse among the mossy boundaries of the dead, inhale the musk of surrounding woods. Many markers unreadable, a few discernible letters or bleached completely bare, just a grainy discoloration where an identity had been.

After weeks of heavy snowfall near the Chilkoot Pass, on April 2, 1898, the weather took a radically warm shift. Several small snowslides that night culminated in the avalanche of Palm Sunday, April 3, when, according to the placard here "the whole mountain roared loose. Victims were found frozen forever in a running position." There are forty-nine markers within the slat-fenced confines of the cemetery, but no one knows the true number of remains here. Some of the largest hemlock in the area grow over this quiet spot—I alone represent the living as I meander along the pathways—and a speckled light surrounds us. The trees at the entrance are astounding—thick-trunked, close, with bare, horizontal arms entangled. Skeletons in twisted embrace. Ladders of bone. I'd never seen hemlock do this anywhere else. When the photos are developed, a soft, ethereal glow amidst the trees is unmistakable, a canopy of suffused light above the reposing dead.

My birthday is April 3. I walk among the ghosts, quiet and commemorative, pondering. A presentiment, perhaps, of . . . warning? Expectation? Responsibility? Slide Cemetery is shaggy, peaceful, beautiful in its fashion. Alms of fern uncurl along its boundary. 120 years have quieted these lost lives. I feel drawn to this place that marks my birth coincident with tragedy. And now, having offered my attention and respect, I'll recover my sprawled bicycle, take a shortcut, dismount to navigate the rutted mud and dung of the private horse path, and be at the homestead in no time. It's turned chilly here in the last half hour. Shadows have spread beneath those entwined branches. Back at the cabin, I'll bathe, stoke the wood-burning stove for the evening, and return to a new novel I saved for the trip. A story of how the dead are ever among us, watchful and abiding.

ॐ

The cold, gray, drizzly weeks of July finally give way to sunshine, and do so dramatically. Consecutive days hit 88°F, and one can feel the collective excitement, an impulse to undress. The Yukoners in their tents and campers will descend on the campground and riverbank by the weekend, but for now it's a solitary paradise. This morning I am wearing shorts and a T-shirt, and—for the only time I will during the entire trip—the sandals that I packed in a moment of idiocy. I have recovered from a cold that laid me out for days. From the West Creek Bridge, on a pebbled island where creek and river merge, three red-breasted mergansers, female, lovely ducks. Then I am leaving footprints along the sandy bank where the Taiya flows closest to the cabin, ten minutes or less by foot.

Recent mornings I've made a ritual of, first thing, walking along the river to spy on a bald eagle nest that overhangs the water. It's been there for years and could be abandoned. Finally, I've seen a sign of life—an adult bird preening on a higher branch. I want to see it again. Approaching me, a woman, barefoot, walking her Yorkshire terrier. We smile. "Best day of the year," she says as we pass, and I can't disagree. No eagle, but it hardly matters. Later, after the day's poem is complete, with the whole fine afternoon selfishly ahead, I will bike to the flats. Of course I will. And there will be eagles.

Biographical Note

Gaylord is the author of sixteen previous books of poetry, fiction, criticism, and cookery, including the poetry collection *Worship the Pig* (Red Hen, 2020) and *The Poet's Guide to Food, Drink, & Desire* (Stephen F. Austin, 2015). His poems have appeared in *Best American Poetry* and *The Bedford Introduction to Literature*. His many international residencies include Hawthornden Castle (Scotland) and the Global Arts Village (India), and he has taught in Russia, Kenya, England, and the Czech Republic. Brewer was awarded a Tennessee Arts Commission Fellowship in 2009. He is a native of Louisville, Kentucky, and has been a professor at Middle Tennessee State University for more than three decades.